AF600332

# Diocesan Faculties

According to

# The Code of Canon Law

## Dissertation

Submitted to the Faculty of Sacred Sciences of
the Catholic University of America
in partial fulfilment of the requirements
for the

DOCTORATE IN CANON LAW

BY THE

REV. HUBERT LOUIS MOTRY, S. T. D., J. C. L.
*Priest of the Diocese of Albany, N. Y.*

The Catholic University of America
Washington, D. C., 1922

Nihil Obstat.

†THOMAS J. SHAHAN,

*Censor deputatus.*

---

Imprimatur.

†MICHAEL J. CURLEY,

*Archiepiscopus Baltimorensis.*

Baltimorae, die 1 Maii, 1922.

# CONTENTS

## *Contents*

## INTRODUCTION

The present dissertation deals with the subject of diocesan faculties as they are directly deducible from the New Code of Canon Law. The study is primarily a theoretical discussion of the basis, nature and extent of exceptional law as implied in the concept of "faculty." However, the highly practical aspect of the subject-matter is not lost sight of, and not infrequently are the principles and statements of the exceptional law shown in their application to facts and contingencies that come within their scope.

Though the matter of the dissertation comes in contact with many questions of a general juridical nature, it is obviously beyond the confines and purpose of the study to enter into a detailed discussion thereof. That must be left to the domain of special treatises.

The work is divided into two parts. The first part is a general discussion of the subject of "faculties," the second treats in particular of the diocesan faculties.

In the first part, a brief historical survey of the origin and development of faculties prefaces the discussion of the juridical concept of the nature, source and extent of faculties. The constituent elements of the concept expressed by the term "faculty" are submitted to a somewhat lengthy inquiry because of the indefinite meanings frequently associated with this term.

The second part of the dissertation submits a list and a discussion of the various concessions that could be placed in the document of diocesan faculties. As indicated above, only those faculties are considered, which, according to the general law, the diocesan priests either possess *ex potestate ordinaria* or may possess *ex potes-*

*tate delegata,* i. e., through the concession of the local Ordinary. Faculties concerning the celebration of Mass and concerning confession receive, for the obvious reasons of their importance and the frequency of their application, a lengthier discussion than others.

Faculties, that could be construed on the basis of regional, provincial or diocesan law, are not submitted to discussion in these pages. Such faculties are usually found in the diocesan statutes that frequently embody, at least in outline, the decrees of plenary and provincial councils and of diocesan synods. These particular powers are to follow, of course, the general regulations of the Code, and consequently may be increased, or are to be diminished or, perhaps, even annulled, as the case may require, unless provision to the contrary has been made by peculiar indults or privileges.

# FIRST PART

## Faculties in General

# CHAPTER I

## Historical Notes

The word "faculty" is etymologically derived from the Latin *facultas* which, in turn, with a modified meaning finds its origin in the term *facilitas*. *Facultas* is best translated with "power," whereas *facilitas* claims "ease" or "readiness" as its first meaning. In the *Ius Civile Romanum* the term *facultas* is used as the equivalent of *Potestas, Copia, Arbitrium.*[1]

When the term *facultas* first occurred in Church Law is a matter of conjecture. It was no doubt applied specifically in the sense in which it is now prefixed to the formulas long before the fifteenth century. In the *Operosum,*[2] 1637, we find the term *facultates* used in a manner that presupposed a set terminological place for it in the Canon Law of that day. In the course of that constitution, it is stated that because of the complaints of bishops and missionaries many clauses were added to or taken from the "old formulas." The term *facultates* is used in several passages without any modifying explicative expression.

If, at a later day, we read in the *Apostolicum Ministerium*[3] that *facultates* are granted by the Holy See to do away with the difficulties that arise in the concession of "*peculiares dispensationes et privilegia*" ("*difficile est Romam confugere*"), we are impressed with the wide scope that the term had then acquired. The close relation of *facultas* and *privilegia* is well brought out by the constitution just mentioned:

*"Cum a Sancta Sede animadversum sit, plurima saepe contingere in regionibus longe dissitis, quibus ut consulatur, peculiares dispensationes et privilegia quandoque opportuna, quandoque etiam ad animarum regimen necessaria requiruntur, ad quae obtinenda difficile est Romam confugere, eadem Sancta Sedes in more habuit, habetque in praesenti, Episcopis in remotioribus Provinciis commorantibus, quasdam facultates impertiri, quibus uti possint vel immediate vel per inferiores Sacerdotes a se designatos."*

For the present it will suffice to say that the term *facultates* no doubt received its prominence from the standard formulas that had appeared long before the time of Urban VIII (1623-1644).

It might be well to add that the above-mentioned *Operosum* plainly shows that the special commission of Cardinals[4] considered the task of reformulating the faculties a matter of vast importance. *"Haec vero deliberatio non longitudine dumtaxat temporis, sed difficultate etiam rei propositae molesta fuit; Deo autem duce, atque sub felici auspicio SSmi. D. N. finem aliquando habuit, totumque negotium post graves et diuturnos labores conclusum . . . coram Sanctissimo die X Februarii 1637 enarratum, atque ipsius Christi Vicarii sententia approbatum fuit."*[5]

In the *"Praefatio in Formulas Facultatum,"* written by the Secretary of the S. C. de Prop. Fide,[6] mention is again made of this special commission or congregation, as it is called in both the *Operosum* and the *Cum ex multiplicatis.* The Secretary's preface states that the *"peculiaris Congregatio"* took almost three years to complete its work of standardizing the formulation of faculties. The older formulas had been given (*"olim"*) by the popes through the Holy Office both before and after the institution of the S. C. de Prop. Fide.

The "*peculiaris congregatio,*" according to the Secretary, found it advisable to adopt a new policy in the formulating of faculties: "*Patribus visum fuit alia via in . . . Formularum compositione esse incedendum.*" They decided to adopt certain general regulations which were to be followed in the granting of faculties. Then, too, they composed general faculties which according to these general regulations could easily be expedited for the various parts of the world with but little trouble, "*modico labore.*"[7]

The principle of prudent conservatism in the formulation of faculties that would not have to be changed at frequent intervals is evident both from the wording of the "*Praefationes*" mentioned above and the established facts of the substantially unchanged status of the faculties, as they have come down to the time of the codification of the present Church Law.[8] In the *Operosum* we read: *Sic enim fiet ut singulares Formulae ex regulis ac normis stabilitis deductae, maiorem et auctoritatis vim, et diuturnitatis firmitatem acquirant.*" The very purpose of the "*peculiaris congregatio*" was to avoid the changeableness and confusion caused by the adding or the taking away of modifying clauses, which gave rise to the admittedly justifiable complaints of bishops and missionaries.

According to Nilles,[9] there were ten standard formulas of ordinary faculties which were numbered with Roman numerals from I to X. Reiffenstuel (died 1703)[10] makes us acquainted with the faculties that had been granted in the year 1696 by the Congregation of the Universal Inquisition to the bishop of Freising, where Reiffenstuel was professor of Canon Law.[11] The faculties granted to this bishop are merely titled: "*Facultates concessae a S. D. N. D. Innocentio Divina Providentia Papa XII Reverendissimo DD. Joanni Francisco Episcopo Frisingensi.*" The word *formula* does not occur at the heading or in the conclusion of the faculties. The faculties, however, are those which, until recently, have been granted under Formula III to the bishops of Germany, Austria, Belgium.[12] According to Nilles, [13] the formulas marked V, VII, VIII and IX were no longer granted at the time his article appeared.[14]

The standardized wording of the faculties is a matter that deserves our attention. If we examine some of the faculties under Formula I, which were granted formerly to bishops in this country, and some of the faculties under Formula III, granted to the bishops of the countries mentioned above, we shall find a striking identity of terms, which will allow us readily to understand the great care and labor bestowed on the original formulation of powers that the pope wished to concede to the bishops in various countries. The "*graves et diuturni labores*" mentioned in the *Operosum*[15] are readily understood after considering that the work of formulating faculties stood the test of several centuries, and that many of the faculties have remained absolutely unchanged up to the present day.[16]

Some formulas of extraordinary faculties are titled with capital letters, such as the extraordinary faculties our bishops used to have (C. D. E.). Some are distinguished by the abbreviation: Extr. with a small single or double letter; e. g., Extr. a, or Extr. aa, or with a capital letter; e. g., Extr. A. Others again have no special sign of distinction and begin with "*ex audientia Sanctissimi.*"[17]

The faculties "pro foro interno" are granted by the Sacred Penitentiary and are known under the title of "*Pagella Facultatum S. Poenitentiariae.*"[18] These faculties were not revoked by the decree, "Proxima sacra," of April 25, 1918, since only those faculties were abrogated, that were given *pro foro externo.*

Their origin, development, and present status are by their very nature and purpose less subject to investigation. In the "*pagella facultatum S. Poen. pro simplic-*

*ibus confessariis*" we read: "*illas* (*scl. facultates*), *nemini manifestes, nisi necessitas aut utilitas id exegerit.*" The greater variety of circumstances in cases of conscience, and the explicit treatment of such cases in moral theology text-books have been to some extent the reason why the faculties for the internal forum have not received as prominent a discussion as the faculties for the external forum. If we compare the "*pagella S. Poen. pro episcopis*" and one of the formulas; e. g., Form. I or Form. C, we shall find a great difference in the length of the articles. Those of the "*pagella*" are substantially longer than those of the formulas. The "*pagella*" for ordinary confessors contains likewise articles of considerable length. The articles make the absolution for the internal forum dependent on the fulfillment of certain conditions and enter into detailed circumstances of the individual case in which power of absolving is petitioned.

## Notes (Chapter I)

1. Cf. Dirksen, *Manuale Iuris Civilis*, p. 364, Berlin, 1887.
2. S. C. Prop. Fide, in Coll. n. 88.
3. Benedict XIV, Constit. 30 May, 1753.
4. Some belonged to the S. C. De Prop. Fide, some to the S. C. Inquisitionis.
5. It seems that Wernz assigns the 10th of Feb. 1637, as the date of the *Operosum*. *Op. cit.* I, p. 213. In the Coll. S. C. de Prop. Fide, n. 88, the only annotation of time given is the year 1637. As appears from the above quotation, the date Feb. 10, 1637 was the exact date on which the work of the special commission for the reformulation of faculties was approved. This approbation and this date are mentioned in the *Operosum*. Hence, the exact date of the appearance of the *Operosum* is not Feb. 10, 1637. Its appearance must be assigned to a later month, most probably of the same year. The *Operosum* is entitled in the Coll. S. C. de Prop. Fide as: *"Praefatio Emi. D. Cardinalis de Cremona in Formulas Facultatum."*
6. *Cum ex multiplicatis*, Coll. S. C. de Prop. Fide, n. 89.
7. For further details cf. Mergentheim, *Die Quinquennalfakultaeten pro foro externo*, II, pp. 60, sqq.
8. Both ordinary and extraordinary faculties underwent certain changes in 1894. Putzer, *Comment. in Facult. Apost.*, p. 4.
9. ZKT, 1891, p. 552.
10. *Ius Canonicum*, t. IV. p. 148, Venetiis, 1785.
11. Cf. Wernz, *op. cit.*, vol. I, p. 442. Also Schulte, *Geschichte der Quellen und Literatur des Canonischen Rechts*, vol. 3, p. 154. Stuttgart, 1880.
12. Putzer, *op. cit.*, p. 4.
13. *Loc. cit.*
14. Cf. Cath. Encyclopedia, vol. V, Article on *Faculties*, by A. B. Meehan.
15. S. C. De Prop. Fide, 1637.
16. We may compare the faculty in art. 23 of Formula I with the faculty in art. 15 of Formula III—incidentally, the longest faculty granted in either formula. The wording in both is exactly the same. Likewise Form I, art. 3, and Form III, art. 13, Form. I, art., and Form III, art. 4.
17. Other details, beyond the scope of the present study, may be found in the author quoted above: Nilles, ZKT, 1891, pp. 552, sqq.
18. Cf. Analecta Ecclestiastica, Vol. IV, p. 459. Also Nouvelle Revue Theologique, vol. XXIV, pp. 631, sqq. American Eccl. Review, vol. XVI, pp. 173, sqq. Le Canoniste Contemporain, vol. XX, 1897, pp. 56, sqq., gives the additions to the former formula in parenthesis. The claim of the "Canoniste" that they are *"additions importantes"* is hardly substantiated.

## CHAPTER II

### Definition

The term "faculty," as it is used in Canon Law, seems to have had no formulated definition before the appearance of Konings-Putzer's *Commentarium in Facultates Apostolicas.* "Faculty" apparently was considered so closely related to "privilege" that no further attention was paid to giving the former a well-outlined and concise interpretation.[1]

The definition given by Putzer[2] is as follows: "*Facultas denotat potestatem, quam superior ecclesiasticus jurisdictione in foro externo praeditus cuidam sibi quoquo modo subdito personaliter concedit, aliquid sive in foro conscientiae tantum sive etiam pro foro externo valide aut licite aut saltem tuto agendi.*[3] Wernz[4] gives practically the same definition: "*Facultas definitur potestas quam superior ecclesiasticus jurisdictione in foro externo praeditus subdito concedit aliquid sive in foro poenitentiali, vel conscientiae tantum, sive etiam pro foro externo valide vel licite aut saltem tuto agendi.*"

Cocchi[5] defines "faculty": *Potestas a legitimo superiore concessa, vi cuius aliquis agere valeat quod per se ad ipsum superiorem spectaret.*

The definition given by Meehan[6] is as follows: "The conferring on a subordinate, by a superior who enjoys jurisdiction in the external forum, of certain ecclesiastical rights which are denied him by common law; to act, namely, in the external or internal forum validly or lawfully, or at least safely." Meehan places more stress upon the act of conferring of faculties than on the concept of faculty. An analysis of the elements in the definition of Putzer, which is practically that of Wernz and Meehan, will bring out a few fine points that are well worth considering.

In the first place, every faculty denotes a *potestas*, which, abstractly considered, partakes of the broader meaning of *ius*. A faculty is a right which is not bound or silenced, but a right that is transferrable under certain conditions into exercise. A right which the possessor may transfer into exercise is, hence, appropriately called a power, *potestas*. The word *potestas* is well chosen, too, in the meaning that a faculty is a communicated superior authority. The authority that is exercised in the use of a faculty is an ability, a capacity, an authorization, derived from a higher governing entity, which communicated authority is equivalent in a true sense to the *potestas superior*.

A faculty, according to the definition given above, must be granted by an ecclesiastical superior who has jurisdiction in the external forum. Here may be added, for the complete interpretation of the term "faculty," the consideration that the *potestas* must be conceded at least *mediate* by an ecclesiastical superior. Not all faculties are conceded *immediate* by ecclesiastical superiors. Some may be granted with the understanding that they are concessible through sub-delegation from one subject to another in equal standing.

Of course, it could be said that in such an instance there is no question of concession but merely of further delegation or sub-delegation. This brings out an element in the concept of faculties which is of fundamental importance. A faculty is at all times a concession of the power of a superior to an inferior. Hence, abstractly speaking, the superior may at any time revoke the concession he has granted. Likewise, he may increase or diminish, modify or condition it as he deems fit. His acts of granting or revoking faculties will always be valid. The opportuneness of the revocation is a question that must look to the circumstances for its substantiation.

The definition states that the superior who granted faculties must have jurisdiction *in foro externo.* At first sight that seems quite plausible. For we think of concessions in terms of powers that are granted for the correct external government of subjects. We think likewise of bishops, or vicars general, who are the immediate grantors of faculties in most cases, even in matters pertaining to the internal forum, as, for instance, in episcopal reservations. However, the definition does not seem to be so thorough on this point. As stated above, Cocchi has sensed the impropriety of this limitation and omitted the restriction from his definition.

In the first place, there is no solid argument why the superior who grants faculties *pro foro interno* should have jurisdiction *in foro externo* also. Of course, the very fact that he is a superior shows a relation to the external forum. Still it is quite conceivable that a grantor of faculties *pro foro interno* could be superior *ad hoc* only. There is no palpable reason why such a superior could not be considered as one with directive powers in the forum of conscience only. The concept of such a superiority would not contain the elements of a power that controls subjects in their external relations to one another and to the common good, although even that element in the usual concept of "superiority" would exist *in causa.* For this "superiority" in the internal forum would have a much more direct and efficacious relation to the individual than the "superiority" of the external forum could ever hope to attain. Hence, the *iudicium sacramentale,* though not shaped in detail as the *iudicium extra-sacramentale,* is a far better instance of what an effective judgment should be.

As a matter of fact, the superior who grants faculties is not always endowed with power or jurisdiction in the *forum externum.* Let us turn to canon 258 of the New Code. There we find the Sacred Tribunal of the Penitentiary constituted as a tribunal, the jurisdiction of which is expressly limited to the *forum internum.* And, as if to do away with any possible doubt about its competency, the concept of its jurisdiction is evolved in detail: The canon, par. 1, reads as follows: "*Sacrae Poenitentiariae praeficitur cardinalis Poenitentiarius Major. Hujus tribunalis iurisdictio coarctatur ad ea quae forum internum, etiam non sacramentale, respiciunt; quare hoc tribunal pro foro interno gratias largitur, absolutiones, dispensationes, commutationes, sanationes, condonationes; excutit praeterea quaestiones conscientiae easque dirimit.*" A more explicit statement, that this grantor of dispensations, etc., has no jurisdiction in the external forum, could not be desired. The Sacred Penitentiary grants the *pagella facultatum* we spoke of above. As the source, from which the faculties *pro foro interno* in certain cases are to be obtained, it has been placed above the confessors of the entire Church. There is no doubt that it is the *superior* that grants or concedes certain faculties *in foro interno.* Still it is not endowed with jurisdiction in the external forum. Hence, it would seem that the definition given by Putzer should be subjected to a revision on this point. There is no reason why the element of superiority with jurisdiction in the external forum need be retained.

The qualification mentioned could be dropped from the definition without any disadvantage to the usual concept of "faculty." As a matter of precision, it should be eliminated, even though the great majority of grantors of faculties are endowed with jurisdiction in the external forum. The very consideration that the principal power constituted by the pope for regulating the exceptional powers of the internal forum is not endowed with jurisdiction in the external forum would speak much in favor of making the concept of mere superiority without any further reference to jurisdiction either *in foro interno* or *externo* a fundamental element in the concept of "faculty." This point may become of considerable import in the explanation of the rules of interpretation of faculties, since the same relation, or element, of faculties has a far-reaching meaning for the validity and licitness of many acts.

Now that we have considered who it is meant by *superior jurisdictione praeditus* we come to an element equally involved, namely, that contained in the term: *subditus.* The definition as given by Putzer is somewhat profuse. It states: "*Superior . . . cuidam sibi quoquo modo subdito personaliter concedit.*"

It is quite obvious that if we use the term *superior* we are obliged, because of the implied status of relationship, to use a corresponding term when speaking of the person to whom the faculties are granted. The subject to whom the faculties are granted is modified as a "*sibi quoquo modo subditus.*" This correctly implies that the *subditus* need not necessarily be a *subditus proprius.* He can be a *subditus* in any form. In the example of a granting of faculties to a visiting priest, or bishop, or archbishop, the ordinary is in some sense a superior of the recipient. The canonical regulation which places *peregrinus* under the jurisdiction of the local ordinary in those matters which pertain to the public good would make a visitor subject to the ordinary in the matter of obtaining faculties (with the exception of visiting cardinals).

Wernz obviates all difficulties of definitely modifying the status of the subject by simply using the term *subditus.* There is some justification for that, from both the general standpoint that so detailed a matter need not be placed among the essentials of a definition, and from the particular viewpoint that the modification of *subditus,* because of the great variety of faculties and numerous kinds of subjects, is a matter that will go far beyond the scope of an ordinary definition. Putzer, too, would seek to obviate the difficulty of an exact modification of *subditus* by using the general and comprehensive expression: "*quoquo modo.*" Though Cocchi's definition does not contain express mention of *subditus,* it is obvious that he refers to a subject of some kind by the mere use of the term: *superior.*

The question of subject is of importance in so far as the question of extra-territorial jurisdiction in matters of faculties is concerned. The formulators of the faculties sensed this problem and hence outlined the territorial extent of the applicability of the powers granted. Such expressions as: "*nec illis (scl. facultatibus) uti possit extra fines suae dioecesis,*"[7] "*presbyteris propriae dioecesis,*"[8] indicate clearly the mind of the Congregation that granted the faculties.[9]

The matter of concession is touched by Putzer in the expression "*personaliter concedit.*" Since the term *personaliter* will admit of some latitude of meaning it might be of some value to know precisely to what extent the element of personal concession enters.

If the term is to be understood as meaning that the faculties are to be granted directly or immediately, it is evident that the question of concession refers only to the next immediate superior, who has granted the faculties, and his immediate subject. It is quite clear, too, that "*personaliter*" does not exclude the sending of faculties by some agent, as a messenger, as the method of concession would still be personal. Most probably, the meaning of "*personaliter,*" as used in Putzer's definition, excludes the origin of faculties by custom or prescription.

The New Code reckons habitual faculties among the privileges *praeter ius.* Applying to faculties the rules that hold good for such privileges, there can be no question that, strictly speaking, faculties could be acquired by legitimate custom or prescription. Canon 63 legislates: *Privilegia acquiri possunt non solum per directam concessionem competentis auctoritatis et per communicationem sed etiam per legitimam consuetudinam aut praescriptionem. Possessio centenaria vel immemorabilis inducit praesumptionem concessi privilegii.* The term "*personaliter*" can be eliminated from the definition of "faculty" without any further question now, since the New Code implies that the element of "*personaliter*" does not pertain to the essential constituents of the concept of "faculty."

The definition of Putzer speaks only of concession whereas the New Code adds "*per communicationem.*" Although in canons 64 sqq., on privileges, the term "*communicatio*" refers to an altogether different concept than the one implied by the term as used in the final articles of the formulas, the one used in the formulas is not necessarily excluded in can. 63, as quoted above. Still in can. 66 of the New Code where express mention is made of "*facultates habituales*" the word "*concessio*" (in noun or adjective form) is used consistently. The concept of concession, therefore, may be retained in the definition of "faculty" provided of course, that "faculty" is understood as modified by the term "habitual."

"*Aliquid sive in foro conscientiae tantum sive etiam pro foro externo valide aut licite aut saltem tuto agendi.*" Thus Putzer.[10] Wernz words his definition somewhat differently: "*Aliquid sive in foro penitentiali vel conscientiae tantum, sive etiam pro foro externo valide vel licite aut saltem tuto agendi.*"[11]

This part of the definition contains the purpose of the concession, namely, the execution of an act done validly, or licitly, or at least safely. The causes that necessitate, or advise, the concession of a faculty are either internal or external to the law affected by the faculty.[12] The internal causes are such that emanate from an impossibility or difficulty inherent to the fulfillment of a law under given circumstances. The external causes are such that affect a) the execution, or, rather, non-execution, of the law by reason of the common good, b) the grantors, or c) the recipients of faculties.

The distinction between internal and external causes for the concession of faculties seems to be more incidental and formal than substantial. After all, the external causes for which faculties are granted affect the very existence and nature of the law, since the law, abstractly speaking, is for the common good of society. If, for example, a faculty were granted merely for the sake of showing the liberality of the grantor, the very act of concession would redound to the good of society ultimately. It is presupposed that in such a case there is no abuse of the power of granting concessions.

The distinction between external and internal causes for the use of faculties might be of some value to the grantor in case of doubt as to the propriety of the concession. If, in the mind of the grantor, the faculty is not concessible because of the lack of a solid objective reason, some reason might perhaps be found in an external cause, such as the one mentioned above, namely, a demonstration of the liberality of the superior, or the reward of a person who deserves acknowledgment on the part of the superiors.

Primarily, of course, the objective value of the cause, for which a dispensation is directly granted, should be taken into consideration. There are certain faculties, which, abstracting from internal or external causes, by the wording of the supreme legislator, demand the fulfillment or presence of certain conditions before the faculty may be applied. In such instances the terms of the faculty make the concession thereof absolutely dependent, as to validity or licitness, on the conditions given.

Instead of the wording *"in foro poenitentiaii vel conscientiae,"* the term suggested by the New Code[13] "*in foro interno sacramentali*" could be substituted. For the sake of comprehensiveness the "*forum internum non sacramentale*" could be included in the definition, but the expression "*forum internum*" alone would suffice as a generic term for both the "*forum internum sacramentale*" and the "*forum internum non-sacramentale.*"

The expression "*valide agendi*" has reference to those acts, the very essence of which are in question when a faculty is being used. The "*licite agendi*" refers to non-essential requirements in connection with the acts just mentioned, or also to such acts in which there is no question of validity, because of the very nature of the case, and in which there is only question of conformity to the will of the legislator, as for instance, in the matter of fasting and abstinence. In other words, *liceitas* and *licentia* refer to two distinct kinds of acts. *Liceitas* would refer to acts in which there is also question of validity. *Licentia* would refer to acts to which the element of validity is altogether extraneous. Putzer hints at this distinction, when he limits *facultas* in its strictest sense to jurisdictional power, and in a less strict sense permits it to embrace permissional grants.[14]

"*Aut saltem tuto agendi.*" Occasionally a doubt will arise as to the sufficiency of a cause in placing a certain act against the law. In order to do away with the worries of conscience, the lawgiver can grant a concession that will change or suspend or abrogate the law in a given case.

The New Code has not given a definition of "faculties." Nor was such to be expected, since definitions usually are not a matter of legislation. However, the Code has given the concept of habitual faculties a definite place in Canon Law. It has thereby given some indication as to how faculties, in general, are to be treated. Canon 66, par. 1, states: *Facultates habituales quae conceduntur vel in perpetuum vel ad praefinitum tempus aut certum numerum casuum, accensentur privilegiis praeter ius.*

Before we proceed any further with the consideration of the meaning of this paragraph of canon 66, we shall have to consider a certain division of privileges, namely, the *privilegia contra ius* and the *privilegia praeter ius.* This division is so important that it enters into the very terminology of the definition of privilege: "*Privilegium—objective spectatum—est lex privata specialem favorem contra vel praeter ius commune concedens, subjective est ius speciale permanens a superiore contra vel praeter ius commune in gratiam concessum.*"[15] It would be beyond the scope of this study to take up this definition or others at length. It will suffice for the present to put down in a few words the accepted meaning of *privilegia praeter ius.*

At first thought, the difference between *praeter* and *contra ius* would appear to be a matter of little import, because all the faculties are *outside* the law, whether they be *beyond* or *against* it. Still, the authors have paid much attention to the distinction for the sake of thoroughness in the discussion of the various kinds of privileges. Reiffenstuel[16] gives a quite clear concept when he says that a *privilegium praeter ius* is granted: "*quando ipsamet materia, seu actus privilegii non est quidem in se iure prohibitus, sed tamen non nisi certis personis concessus.*" Schmalzgrueber[17] defines a *privilegium praeter ius:* "*quod concedit favores peculiares in iure non expressos, veluti est potestas absolvendi a reservatis, dispensandi, etc.*"

Wernz[18] calls Hinschius to task for discounting the division of privileges into those *contra* and those *praeter ius.* Hinschius, he claims, bases the denial of the distinction on the assumption that there is only one class of privileges in existence, namely, those *contra ius.* Wernz brings a solid reason for upholding the distinction:

*"Nam multae facultates absolvendi vel dispensandi, quae conceduntur praeter ius, non contra ius, merito dicuntur privilegia, quia constituunt leges privatas concedentes specialem favorem, licet minus strictum.*"[19]

The New Code takes no special stand on the discussion of the distinction between privileges, faculties, and dispensations, but it does imply strongly that it accepts the opinion proposed by Wernz. The code goes no further than to say that the "*facultates habituales accensentur privilegiis praeter ius.*" It has, however, approved of the traditional classification of privileges "*praeter ius.*" The Code has not given us a definition of "faculty," but it has indicated the nature thereof enough to assist in the correct interpretation of the powers granted under the title of faculties.

After all that has been said in the preceding pages about the various elements that enter the definition of "faculty" the following definition based on the concepts offered by Putzer and Wernz is submitted for consideration: "*Facultas est potestas quam superior ecclesiasticus, jurisdictione in foro respectivo praeditus, subdito concedit ad ponendum vel omittendum actum praeter vel contra ius valide, aut licite aut saltem tuto.* The classification of faculties "*contra ius*" is mentioned merely for the sake of comprehending the exceptional cases in which faculties grant a power that is really against the law, such as the exemption from the *cathedraticum.*

It is to be recalled that the Code speaks only of those faculties that are "*habituales.* The definition just given applies both to habitual and transitory, or actual, faculties. The habitual faculties mentioned in canon 66 are those that are conceded by the Holy See.

The discussion among the authors as to whether the pope only can grant *privilegia praeter ius* is well worth recalling here in connection with habitual faculties. Since general habitual faculties are granted by the Holy

See only, and as such are considered among *privilegia praeter ius,* we may surmise that the Code leans towards the opinion which upholds the affirmative side in the question mentioned.

Ballerini-Palmieri[20] upholds the affirmative opinion with the argument: *"Solus legislator seu supremus princeps communitatis potest alicui facultatem talem concedere agendi praeter legem (i. e. generalem), ut ea sit juridica, et universa communitas teneatur eam servare privilegiàto."* Wernz[21] thoroughly approves of this opinion.

Bishops, in centuries past, had the power of instituting new feasts, irregularities, marriage impediments, and consequently had the power of granting faculties concerning the non-observance, or dispensations, in such matters. But with the development of church organization there came a closer contact between the various parts of the Church and its head, which necessitated a centralization of power and a unifying system. Matters of Church discipline had to be regulated from one central organization for the sake of unity. The affirmative side, which seems to be the only tenable opinion in this question, should stress that fact in treating the historical development of the reservations of certain episcopal powers to the Holy See. If the limitations, now existing and established by common law, have not been in force from the beginning of the Church, that condition was due, not to a principle according to which bishops in their dioceses would have an inherent right to such powers, but to the deficiencies that are to be found in a developing organization, such as was the Church.

The question here proposed regarding the concession of *privilegia praeter ius* is very closely allied with the question concerning the conferring of episcopal jurisdiction. Wernz treats this question extensively in his treatise *"De Episcopis."*[22] There seems to be no reasonable objection against the opinion which holds that the "particular jurisdiction which the individual bishops exercise over their dioceses is not derived immediately from God, but from the Roman Pontiff as from the proximate cause." However, this question is more of dogmatic than canonical value.[23]

## Notes (Chapter II)

1. AKR, 1901, p. 287.
2. Laurentius in AKR, *loc. cit.*, wrongly attributes the definition of "*facultas*" to Konings. It was Putzer who prefixed the general treatise on faculties to Konings' Commentary, and formulated the definition. Compare Konings' *Commentarium* edited in 1884, and the third edition thereof in 1893.
3. Putzer, *op. cit.*, p. 1.
4. *Op. cit.* I, p. 212.
5. *Commentarium in Codicem Juris Canonici,* Turin, 1920, p. 171.
6. Cath. Encycl., vol. V, p. 748.
7. Form. I, art. 29, Form. C, art. 13.
8. Form D. E.
9. The New Code settles some of the difficulties that arise in connection with "*subditus*" in its canons on jurisdiction. For an extensive treatment of the topic of jurisdiction we must refer to textbooks that treat of this subject.
10. *Op. cit.* p. 1.
11. *Op. cit.* I, p. 212.
12. Cf. Noldin, *Summa Theol. Mor.*, vol. I, pp. 211, sqq. Innsbruck, 1914.
13. Can. 1047.
14. Putzer, *op. cit.*, p. 2.
15. Wernz, *op. cit.* I, p. 195.
16. *Ius Canonicum Universum,* t. V, p. 278.
17. *Ius Ecclesiasticum Universum,* t. V, pars. III, tit. XXXIII, n. 57, p. 85.
18. *Op. cit.*, vol. I, p. 197, in footnote 15.
19. *Loc. cit.*, in footnote, vol. I, p. 198.
20. *Op. Theol. Moralis,* vol. I, p. 428.
21. *Op. cit.*, vol. I, pp. 199, sqq.
22. *Op. cit.*, vol. II, pars. II, n. 737.
23. For opposite opinion, cf. Bartmann, *Lehrbuch der Dogmatik,* p. 584.

## CHAPTER III

### Divisions

There are several divisions of faculties according to the various points from which they may be considered. We may first consider faculties as to their *objective contents.* Thus we have the faculties: (a) that are jurisdictional, namely such upon the exercise or use of which the validity of certain acts depends; (b) that are called *gratiae* or *licentiae;*[1] (c) that are given *ad cautelam.* This threefold division is contained in the definition which treats of the purpose of faculties: *"ad agendum valide, vel licite, vel saltem tuto."* Putzer claims, and rightly so, that only the first of these classes deserves the term "faculties." It is obvious that the primary meaning of faculty is power, a capacity to act. It is only in a secondary sense that the term faculty means a permission *"ad licite agendum."* The third division has still less claim to being called "faculty," because in reality, it is not even a permission in the usual sense but rather an assurance to the doubting agent that the act to be carried out or the omission thereof, as the case may be, receives the approval of authority. In certain instances, however, the faculty *"ad cautelam"* or *"ad agendum tuto"* may become a full fledged faculty, namely, then when objectively the conditions for the validity of an act are wanting, and the faculty granted supplies the deficiency.

This division serves to bring out the difficulty in mapping out the territory that belongs to dispensational faculties. Authors are not agreed as to whether a dispensation can be called a *privilegium praeter* or *contra ius.* Schmalzgrueber places dispensations under the heading of *privilegia praeter ius.*[2] Pirrhing states with some diffidence: "*Videtur dispensatio a privilegio contra ius non differe.*"[3] Reiffenstuel complicates the question somewhat by adding a new term: "*Aliud* (*privilegium*) *praeter ius sive* (*ut alii loquuntur*) *utlra ius: v. g. potestas . . . dispensandi.*" They differ in this, he claims, that the *privilegia contra ius* are to be strictly interpreted, while those *praeter ius* may receive a mild construction, "*cum sint merae gratiae ac beneficia principis.*"[4] Evidently there is a lack of harmony in determining what the concepts *praeter ius* and *contra ius* precisely mean.

As stated above, Wernz rightly objects to Hinchius' complete denial of the distinction. Even though there is some misunderstanding among authors on this point, the general assertion of a division persists, and the allocation of dispensations under one or the other heading among authors finds its justification in the respective author's view on the extent of a concession beyond the law. Wernz seems to insinuate some common ground for a compromise: "*Nam multae facultates absolvendi vel dispensandi, quae conceduntur praeter ius, non contra ius, merito dicuntur privilegia, quia constituunt leges privatas concedentes specialem favorem, licet minus strictum.*"[5]

The New Code assigns a special title to dispensations.[6] There is apparently no indication that the Code considers the question of a precise demarcation between *privilegia praeter ius* and *privilegia contra ius* worthy of a decision, though there are several terms in this title and in the one on privileges, the consideration of which will help somewhat to gain a clearer concept of faculties.

In can. 66, par. 1, "*facultates habituales,*" are counted among "*privilegia praeter ius.*" In the second paragraph of the same canon we find mention made of the "facultas dispensandi." This obviously is in conformity with the express opinion of Schmalzgrueber and

Reiffenstuel. Another indication of the attitude of the Code toward the question is to be found in the canons that treat of the interpretation of faculties, which will be taken up in a later chapter.

*Ratione subjecti concedentis,* we find faculties divided into those that are granted by the supreme authority, namely the Pope, either personally or through one of the congregations or the Penitential Tribunal,[7] and those that are granted by Ordinaries. *Praelati Regulares* are also among those who have the power of granting faculties.

Other divisions, such as general and particular, are self-explanatory, since they reflect merely the scope, or purpose, of the concession granted.

The *formulas,* too, which we have mentioned in a preceding chapter remind us of the division of faculties, ordinary and extraordinary. These terms are sanctioned as meaning only those faculties which emanate from Rome.[8]

A division worthy of mention here is that of the faculties *pro foro externo* and *interno,* and *pro utroque foro.*

A division of more practical than theoretical value is that of matrimonial and non-matrimonial faculties. Peculiar as this division may seem, it finds its ready application in the extraordinary faculties. The former extraordinary faculties in formulas D and E are matrimonial only, while none of the faculties in formula C refer to matrimony. The faculties granted in the *Proxima sacra*[9] are likewise matrimonial only.

The Code indicates a distinction of *habitual* and (*actual*) *transitory* faculties. According to the express statement of can. 66 there are faculties granted "*in perpetuum,*" "*ad praefinitum tempus*" and "*ad certum numerum casuum.*" Canon 85 speaks of a "*facultas concessa ad certum casum.*" Canon 86 indicates still another kind: "*dispensatio quae tractum successivum habet,*" e. g. a dispensation from fasting for the season of Lent.

The *Proxima sacra*[10] speaks of faculties with which the "*Ordinarii locorum*" are supplied "*ipso iure.*" The same decree speaks of faculties "*ad decennium, ad quinquennium,*" and "*ad triennium,*" and of the *Breve* of twenty-five years. Indult and faculty are synonymous terms in the *Proxima Sacra.* The word "indult" has as yet a still less fixed usage in canon law than "faculty." There seems to be a modifying quality attached, which would make the use of the term "indult" applicable *usually* in instances where large numbers of recipients are concerned. Putzer implies this when he says: "*si generales sunt* (*i. e. facultates*) *etiam 'Indultorum' nomine cognoscuntur.*"[11] Thus we speak of an indult in the matter of fast and abstinence when there is question of a great number who participate in the indult. The term is used, however, also for individual concessions.[12]

## Notes (Chapter III)

1. Wernz, *op. cit.*, I, p. 212; Putzer, *op. cit.*, p. 2.
2. *Op. cit.*, V, tit. 33, n. 57.
3. *Ius Canonicum*, 1, V, tit. XXXIII, sec. I, par. 1, n. 5.
4. *Op. cit.*, 1, V, tit. XXXIII, Par. 1, n. 7.
5. *Op. cit.*, I, p. 198, footnote 15.
6. Canons 80 to 86.
7. Cf. Ojetti, *De Romana Curia*, Rome, 1910, pp. 11, 112, 169, sqq.
8. Cf. Augustine, *A Commentary on Canon Law*, vol. I, p. 159, footnote 11.
9. S. C. Cons., April 25, 1918.
10. S. C. Cons., April 25, 1918.
11. *Op. cit.*, p. 2.
12. Cf. e. g. can. 638.

## CHAPTER IV

### Interpretation of Faculties

The New Code has laid down certain rules according to which faculties are to be interpreted. These rules, however, are few in number. The Code evidently presupposes that the interpretation of faculties will follow the general lines indicated by the interpretation placed upon church law, rescripts and privileges.[1]

Perhaps, the most general rule of interpretation applicable to faculties lies in canon 67 of the Code, which, however, speaks in first line of privileges. Still, since faculties are listed among privileges, they should follow the interpretation of privileges: "*Privilegium ex ipsius tenore aestimandum est, nec licet illud extendere aut restringere.*" Can. 67. On the surface this rule seems to be very commonplace, but upon closer consideration we find that it is a well chosen caution—rather than a regulation—to avoid an excessive interpretation of the power granted. An instance of its application is to be found in the response of the S. R. C. Feb. 27, 1883, in which it was stated that privileges granted for the Archdiocese of Cincinnati concerning the recitation of the Divine Office were not to be extended to the seven other dioceses that were using the same Ordo as the archdiocese. Explanatory of this general principle is also *Regula Iuris 28 in 6to: "Quae a jure communi exorbitant, nequaquam ad consequentiam sunt trahenda."*[2] *Regula iuris 74 in 6to* is likewise to the point: *"Quod alicui gratiose conceditur trahi non debet ab aliis in exemplum."*[3]

Consideration of the attitude of common law towards exceptions has led authors to adopt a general rule which has received, with some variations in terms that are at the same time corrective and explanatory, the sanction of the New Code.[4] The rule of the authors reads as follows: "*Facultates comprehensive non vero extensive interpretandae sunt.*"[5]

The term *comprehensive* and *extensive* refer to the tenor of the concession. Faculties, in other words, are to be interpreted *according* to their contents, and *not beyond* them. A general faculty comprehends all the various species of dispensations that come under the respective genus, but the faculty cannot be applied to another genus, or to a species under that genus. To make the distinction clear, we may consider faculties that are granted for absolution from punishments. If a general faculty is granted to absolve from censures reserved to a superior, the faculty comprehends all the species of censures, but it does not comprehend vindictive punishments of any kind. That is the meaning which the Code has summed up in the axiomatic canon: "*Privilegium* (and faculties are such) *ex ipsius tenore aestimandum est, nec licet illud extendere aut restringere.*" The last clause of this canon "*aut restringere*" is meant obviously for those who would deprive the recipient of the permissible exercise of his privilege.

It is therefore in accordance with the juridical concept of faculties to interpret them according to their terms, and all that they imply. If the faculties are general in their terminology the grantor is rightly supposed to have conferred upon the recipient all that may be understood by the broad terms used in the concession. Exceptions will be considered later. General or broad faculties still have their limitations, which are implied or expressed by the very terms that are general. A certain territory or field of interpretability is allowed. Beyond that, however, the terms do not extend. No matter how general the terms of a faculty are, it is not permissible to apply the power granted to cases not contained in the concession, nor to persons not included therein. If, for instance, a faculty of very broad terms is granted that is applicable to the clergy only, it would be a flagrant violation of this first rule to interpret the faculty as comprehending also the laity.

The *comprehensive* interpretation of faculties admits of a broad and a strict sense.[6] A broad comprehensive interpretation is applicable when the faculty is granted for persons not determined in name or in number. This is, of course, merely another view of the rule that general terms may be interpreted in a general way.

A *strict comprehensive* interpretation is to be used in these instances when faculties are granted for specified persons or cases. While in the *broad comprehensive* interpretation a faculty comprehends all those who may be classified under its general terms, a faculty that is granted for specified persons or cases comprehends only those mentioned implicitly or explicitly in the terms.

To the *broad comprehensive* interpretation there are some exceptions. *Regula Iuris 81 in 6to* reads: *"In generali concessione non veniunt ea quae quis non esset verisimiliter in specie concessurus."* D'Annibale adds also the exceptions constituted by custom or law.[7] Thus, in the ordinary faculties granted by bishops to confessors the *"facultas absolvendi a peccatis"* does not include reserved cases. Nor does the papal faculty to absolve from censures reserved *simpliciter* to the Holy See include the power to absolve from censures reserved *specialiter* to same.

As to general faculties, they may be interpreted *extensive* if there is a common and constant teaching among authors favoring such an interpretation, or if the extension of a faculty is practically the comprehension thereof. This latter exception would seem to hold good even then when faculties are given for specific persons and specific cases. D'Annibale states[8] that no faculty is to be interpreted so as to become burdensome or useless to the recipient, and if it were useless, unless another dispensation were applied, this second dispensation would be considered as tacitly granted. Thus, in the example adduced in D'Annibale's footnote to n. 234, a dispensation granted to a cleric in major orders for contracting marriage would absolve him likewise from the obligation of reciting the Divine Office.

In case of doubt as to how a faculty is to be interpreted, we find some helpful indication of a solution in canons 68 and 85, both of which refer us back to canon 50. Canon 68 reads as follows: *In dubio privilegia interpretanda sunt ad normam can. 50; sed ea semper adhibenda interpretatio, ut privilegio aucti aliquam ex indulgentia concedentis videantur gratiam consecuti.* Canon 85 states: *Strictae subest interpretatiioni non solum dispensatio ad normam can. 50, sed ipsamet facultas dispensandi ad certum casum concessa.*

The canon referred to deals with rescripts, but it indicates the norm which, according to the Code itself, should guide us in the interpretation of privileges (hence also faculties) and dispensations. The norm there stated prescribes a strict interpretation in matters of litigation, in the encroachment upon the rights of others, in making exceptions to the law for private benefit, and in the obtaining of ecclesiastical benefices. Canon 50 reads: *In dubio, rescripta guae ad lites referuntur vel iura aliis quaesita laedunt, vel adversantur legi in commodum privatorum, vel denique impetrata fuerunt ad beneficii ecclesiastici assecutionem, strictam interpretationem recipiunt; cetera omnia latam.*

The various restrictions placed on interpretations are best summed up in *Regula Iuris 48 in 6to*: *Locupletari non debet aliquis cum alterius iniuria vel iactura.*

The reference in the footnotes of the Code to c. 15, 32, 40, X, *de officio et potestate judicis delegati,* I. 29, forbids the extension of powers conceded beyond the limits of the mandates. In Chapter 15 just noted, the express statement is made: *non est nostrae intentionis dioecesano episcopo . . . praeiudicium generare.* The other references[9] deal principally with the obtaining of ecclesiastical benefices.

It is quite logical that in matters under litigation a faculty with a broad interpretation could interfere seriously with the course of justice. Likewise, in the field of rights acquired by others, the sense of justice forbids an excessive interpretation. It is presupposed that the grantor of powers does not allow his subjects to interfere with one another's rights. Such would be the status, however, if prior grants of rights or powers were disregarded by grants of a later date. Here we naturally apply the *Regula Iuris 54 in 6to*: *Qui prior est tempore, potior est iure.* The third consideration in the norm of can. 50 is the common good. Privileges, or faculties, which would be interpreted adversely to the general law, and that, too, for private convenience only, would again work an injustice. It is ordinarily a question of justice in the fourth restriction also, namely, in the obtaining of benefices, as may be easily deduced from the very nature of the matter.

A general faculty would permit of a general interpretation, as stated above, and that of a broad comprehensive nature. As also stated above, a faculty granted for one specific case must be interpreted in a comprehensive way, true enough, but nevertheless strictly. Cocchi,[10] in explaining can. 67, states: "*privilegia . . . tantum declarative interpretanda sunt ex tenore contra sententiam aliquorum extensivam interpretationem admittentium pro casu similitudinis rationis, nempe docentes extendi posse privilegium a casu ad casum quando par est ratio.* This does not refer, of course, to the opinion: *extensive licet facultates generaliter sonantes interpretari, si pro aliquo casu id fert constans omnium doctorum sententia.*[11] Canon 85 is supplementary to canon 67.

It is to be added that according to canon 68 such an interpretation is to be given at all times that the recipients of faculties derive some benefit from the concession. It would be against prudence if a superior granted a faculty, the interpretation of which would be hemmed in on all sides by so many restrictions that absolutely no advantage could be derived therefrom. A grantor of faculties presupposedly considers the element of advantage or benefit as inherent in every concession. Hence the provision in canon 68: *sed ea semper adhibenda interpretatio, ut privilegio aucti aliquam ex indulgentia concedentis videantur gratiam consecuti.*[12]

In treating of interpretation, the authors lay stress on the *"stylus et praxis vigens Curiae Romanae."* Though the Code does not mention the *"stylus et praxis Curiae Romanae"* in the titles on privileges and dispensation, it does give the style and practice of the Roman Curia a prominent part of can. 20: *Si certa de re desit expressum praescriptum legis sive generalis sive particularis, norma sumenda est, nisi agatur de poenis applicandis, a legibus latis in similibus; a generalibus iuris principiis cum aequitate canonica servatis; a stylo et praxi Curiae Romanae; a cummuni constantique sententia doctorum.* The application of this canon to faculties is quite patent. Faculties are in a true sense particular laws, since as privileges they are *leges privatae.* Even if this point were not urged, it is evident that faculties should be interpreted according to the same standards as the common laws, since faculties are exceptions to the laws.[13] Laws and their exceptions would be a hopeless mass of entangled words if there were no common standard of terms and application.

Canon 42 establishes a principle concerning the importance of the *stylus curiae* which is of value: *Reticentia veri, seu subreptio in precibus non obstat quominus rescriptum vim habeat ratumque sit, dummodo expressa fuerint quae de stylo curiae sunt ad validitatem exprimenda.* Beyond a doubt both the style and the practice of the Curia Romana should serve as the models for diocesan curiae.

In the matter of papal faculties the clauses especially that are used by the Roman Curia in expediting concessions are of great importance. These clauses are divided into two classes: *substantial,* namely, such that affect the validity of a faculty, or dispensation; *non-substantial,* namely such that serve to explain or state the concession more exactly. The qualification that places the clauses in the one class or the other depends on the tenor of the concession granted. The interpretation of the various clauses could and should follow the rules outlined in the Code for rescripts, especially canons 39, 40, 42. The full value of the clauses would have to be left to the explanation of the individual faculty, except, perhaps, those expressions which are general and occur frequently. Such would find an appropriate place for interpretation in the introductory explanation of the various formulas.

## Notes (Chapter IV)

1. Wernz, *op. cit.*, p. 216.
2. Cf. Reifenstuel, t. VI, pp. 48, sqq. where the various opinions and exceptions are treated extensively. Cf. also his explanation of Reg. 15: "*Odia restringi, et favores convenit ampliari.*" *Op. cit.*, pp. 32, sqq.
3. Cf. Reifenstuel, *op. cit.*, pp. 109, sqq.
4. In the canon quoted above, can. 67, and in can. 65.
5. Wernz, *op. cit.*, p. 216; Putzer, *op. cit.*, p. 11.
6. Cf. Putzer, *op cit.*, p. 11, sqq.
7. D'Anniblae, *Summula Theologiae Moralis*, vol. I, n. 228.
8. *Op. cit.*, p. 222.
9. Footnotes attached to canon 50.
10. *Op. cit.*, p. 176.
11. Putzer, *op. cit.*, p. 14.
12. Cocchi, *op. cit.*, p. 176.
13. Cf. Wernz, *op. cit.*, p. 216: *Quoad interpretationem facultatum attendendae sunt generales normae de interpretatione legum ecclesiasticarum.*

# CHAPTER V

## Source and Application of Faculties

The origin or source of faculties may be considered from various angles. The superiors from whom the faculties proceed, have already been mentioned in the division of faculties, namely: the Roman Pontiff (personally or through the congregations or the Tribunal of the Sacred Penitentiary), the Ordinaries and the Religious Superiors.

The immediate agents of the Holy Father in the matter of faculties are the Sacred Congregations and the Tribunal of the Sacred Penitentiary. Their jurisdiction is, of course, ordinary.

Recourse must first be had to the Ordinary (the bishop of the diocese, the vicar general, or *sede vacante* to the administrator or in certain instances to the Apostolic Delegate), who has either ordinary or delegated faculties. If the faculty required goes beyond the jurisdiction of the superior appealed to, recourse must be had ultimately to Rome, usually through the agency of an immediate superior.

The competency of the various Sacred Congregations (and the Sacred Penitentiary for faculties of the internal forum) is plainly stated in the canons of the Code on the Roman Curia. The request for a faculty should be directed according to the jurisdictional or permissional powers residing in the individual Congregation (or Tribunal). Formulas for application in the various cases may be found in text-books, that give practical references to this matter.

In the obtaining of faculties the regulations concerning rescripts must be observed. We have already referred to one of the most important canons on rescripts in a former chapter, namely to canon 50. As the need arises reference will be made to rescript-elements that enter into the discussion of faculties.

Another source of faculties is custom or prescription. Faculties can arise from such customs only which are not expressly reprobated by the Code.

In connection with the source of faculties it will be appropriate to treat, at least briefly, of canons 81, 82, 83. Ordinaries cannot dispense from general laws of the Church, not even in a particular case, unless (a) power for such dispensation has been granted in explicit or implicit terms, or (b) recourse to the Holy See is difficult. The difficulty of recourse is qualified by the condition of serious danger in delay. Moreover, the case must be one in which the Holy See dispenses. Thus canon 81: *A generalibus Ecclesiae legibus Ordinarii infra Romanum Pontificem dispensare nequeunt, ne in casu quidem peculiari, nisi haec potestas eisdem fuerit explicite vel implicite concessa, aut nisi difficilis sit recursus ad Sanctam Sedem et simul in mora sit periculum gravis damni, et de dispensatione agatur quae a Sede Apostolica concedi solet.*

The canon refers in the first place to "general laws" of the Church. The word *general* is used synonymously for *universal* in contradistinction to *particular, peculiar* (see canon 83), *territorial or local.*[1] The power of the *Ordinarii locorum* as to laws that are not general is treated in canon 82. There is no reason why any exception should be made in the interpretation of *general* laws, once the conditions of can. 81 are complied with in the granting of a dispensation. Hence, matrimonial dispensations given according to the norm of can. 81 would be both valid and licit. It must be noted, however, that the end of the law would be frustrated if no provision were made to avoid an enervatingly frequent recurrence of dispensations based on too liberal an interpretation of the lawgiver's generosity. Such provision is made, at times, by application for general faculties, but better still by the adoption of such means that further respect for the strength of the laws, to which exceptions are asked. The former provision, namely, the granting of general faculties, is readily used by the Church in matters of frailty and frequence, the latter in cases where ease of observance and importance of purpose go hand in hand.

"*Ordinarii infra Romanum Pontificem.*" The mention of the Roman Pontiff has more doctrinal than canonical value, because as supreme legislator of the Church he obviously has the power of dispensing in his own laws. This principle, namely, that the lawgiver (or his successor) can dispense in matters of his own laws is stated in can. 80.

It must be noted that *ordinarii* is used without *loci* or *locorum.* Hence, all ordinaries mentioned in can. 198 are included.

The term *nequeunt* is usually associated with the question of validity. It would seem highly improbable that the meaning of the term in canon 81 should extend itself only to *liceitas* or *licentia.* The very purpose and burden of the canon points to the question of validity. The terminology employed in the canons following places the matter beyond a doubt.[2]

"*Ne in casu quidem peculiari*" shows how far this law is to be extended. No exception is to be made beyond those indicated in the canon itself. It is hardly probable that all the clauses following are subordinate to "*ne in casu quidem peculiari,*" unless "*casus peculiaris*" receives a broad interpretation.

"*Nisi haec potestas eisdem fuerit explicite vel implicite concessa.*" The concession of explicit or implicit powers may be made by the Holy See or by common law.[3]

*"Aut nisi difficilis sit recursus ad Sanctam Sedem."* What really constitutes *"difficilis recursus"* is a matter that must be left to the judgment of the Ordinary. There are conditions in which the general public would consider recourse difficult, as for instance, during the recent World War. The authors do not enter into a detailed discussion of the element of *"difficilis recursus,"* most probably for the reason that the difficulty of recourse is dependent on numerous and varied circumstances in the various countries. Recourse need not be accepted in any other than the ordinary sense, namely, in person or by mail.[4] Registered mail does not seem to be an extraordinary means.

The "Holy See" is extensively explained in canon 7: *"Nomine Sedis Apostolicae vel Sanctae Sedis in hoc Codice veniunt non solum Romanus Pontifex, sed etiam, nisi ex rei natura vel sermonis contextu aliud appareat, Congregationes, Tribunalia, Officia, per quae idem Romanus Pontifex negotia Ecclesiae universae expedire solet."*

*"Et simul in mora sit periculum gravis damni."* This condition speaks of "danger." Hence it is not necessary that the *"grave damnum"* be a reality. A probability of weight would suffice. An imprudent fear of supposedly impending evils would not constitute the *"periculum"* mentioned in this canon. The *"damnum"* must be serious, since it is the objective reason for making the exception to a "general law."

*"Et de dispensatione agatur quae a Sede Apostolica concedi solet."* Unusual grants do not come under this heading. Augustine[5] gives an example in which Rome would ordinarily not dispense, namely, in the irregularity *"ex defectu corporis enormi."*

Canon 82 states the power of bishops and *"ordinarii locorum"* as to laws of the diocese, of provincial and plenary councils, with the restriction mentioned in can. 291, par. 2.

In these laws they can dispense, but not in the laws that the Roman Pontiff has made effective for their territory. Such laws could suffer an exception only according to the norm of can. 81.

*Parochi,* according to canon 83, cannot dispense in general or particular laws unless expressly empowered to do so. Canons 1044, 1045, par. 3, 1245, par. 1, are instances in which the power of dispensation has been expressly granted to *parochi.*

The source of dispensation must, as insinuated in a preceding chapter, have a cause corresponding in gravity to the importance of the laws. *"Alias dispensatio ab inferiore data illicita et invalida est."*[6] This canon likewise legislates that a dispensation with a doubt about the sufficiency of the cause may be licitly asked for and both licitly and validitly granted.

In treating of the interpretation of faculties in a preceding chapter we have stated various principles that are to be followed in the practical application of faculties. Here we need add but a few[7] remarks concerning the execution *"in praxi"* of powers granted.

Recipients of faculties must be members of the Church, who are negatively qualified as not expressly excluded by law from receiving grants.[8] They must of course meet the conditions laid down in the grant of the faculty. The faculty can be applied to a *subditus* only. *Vagi* and *pergrini* may become *subditi* by reason of the territorial element.

The act of applying a faculty may take place even when either the grantor or the recipient, or both are absent from their territory. Canon 201, par. 3, settles the dispute that once engaged the authors on the question of territory in the use of a faculty. The faculty of reading forbidden books was confined, by some authors, in its use to the territory of the grantor or executor.[9] The wording of can. 201, par. 3: *"potestatem iurisdic-*

*tionis voluntariam quis exercere potest in—subditum a territorio absentem"* would receive an unwarranted restriction if the faculty of reading forbidden books were excepted.

Wernz adds a word of advice for the use of faculties: "*Denique facultatum usus fiat ex iusta causa et cum debita forma, sine rigore et laxismo meroque arbitrio.*"[10]

## Notes (Chapter V)

### CHAPTER V

1. Cf. Sebastian, *Summarium Theol. Mor.* p. 9. Also Augustine, *op. cit.*, vol. I, p. 89.
2. Compare canons 82, 83.
3. Concessions granted by common law are, for instance the powers granted by canons 990, par. 1, 1043, 1045, pars. 1, 2, 1245, pars. 1, 2, 2237. Cf. Cocchi, *op. cit.*, p. 192, sqq.
4. Augustine, *op. cit.*, p. 177.
5. *Op. cit.*, p. 177.
6. Canon 84.
7. Wernz, *op. cit.*, pp. 215, sqq.
8. Compare canon 36.
9. Cf. Putzer, *op. cit.*, p. 75, Zitelli, *Apparatus Juris Eccl.* p. 59, in footnote. Wernz. *op. cit.*, I, p. 216, footnote 116.
10. *Op. cit.*, I, p. 216.

## CHAPTER VI

### Continuation and Cessation of Faculties

The Code makes express provision for the continuation of habitual faculties *"resoluto iure Ordinarii cui concessae sunt."* Canon 66, par. 2, legislates as follows: *"Nisi in earum concessione electa fuerit industria personae aut aliud expresse cautum sit, facultates habituales, Episcopo aliisve de quibus in can. 198, par. 1, ab Apostolica Sede concessae non evanescunt, resoluto iure Ordinarii cui concessae sunt, etiamsi ipse eas exsequi coeperit, sed transeunt ad Ordinarios qui ipsi in regimine succedunt: item concessae Episcopo competunt quoque Vicario Generali."*

*Regula iuris 46 in 6to* is worthy of quotation here: *"Is, qui in ius succedit alterius, eo iure, quo ille uti debebit."* In as far as faculties are not a strict *ius* the application of this rule to the continuation of faculties would not stand the test of objections. Still, in a broad sense, the rule is the foundation of canon 66, par. 2. A decree of the Holy Office, November 24, 1897, placed the matter of continuation beyond question and the substance of this decree, with a few modifications taken from decisions of a later date, constitute the legislation of can. 66, par. 2. The decree of the Holy Office legislates: *Facultates omnes speciales habitualiter a S. Sede Episcopis aliorumque locorum Ordinariis concessas non suspendi vel desinere ob eorum mortem vel muneris cessationem, sed ad successores Ordinarios transire.*

It is well worth mentioning that the *coetus consultorum dioecesanorum* enjoys in the time preceding the election or appointment of an administrator, the title of

"Ordinary" and, hence, according to canon 66, par. 2, can exercise the powers of habitual faculties. The method to be used in granting faculties by the consultors would be the one suggested in canon 101.[1]

The general tenor of the can. 66, par. 2, is prefaced by the condition *"nisi in earum (scl. facultatum habitualium) concessione electa fuerit industria personae aut aliud expresse cautum sit." Personal* faculties are not transferred *ipso iure* to successors, but only *real* or *non-personal* faculties. Likewise, as is obvious, if an express clause is added, to the effect that certain faculties expire with the person, the successor does not inherit those powers of his predecessor. Faculties granted by the Ordinary do not expire with his death or removal from office, as is deducible from can. 61: *"Per Apostolicae Sedis aut diocesis vacationem nullum eiusdem Sedis Apostolicae aut Ordinarii rescriptum perimitur, nisi aliud ex additis clausulis appareat, aut rescriptum contineat potestatem alicui factam concedendi gratiam peculiaribus personis in eodem expressis, et res adhuc integra sit."*

The **cessation** of faculties takes place in various ways. Canon 61 just quoted implies that, generally speaking, faculties do not expire *resoluto iure delegantis.* However, certain *additae clausulae* could cause the faculties to expire. Such a clause is mentioned in canon 73: *Resoluto iure concedentis, privilegia non exstinguuntur, nisi data fuerint cum clausula: ad beneplacitum nostrum, vel alia aequipollenti.* If, therefore, faculties are granted by the Ordinary with a clause equivalent to the one mentioned in can. 73, the faculties expire with the death of the Ordinary. Hence, faculties granted *ad revocationem nostram,* cease at the death of the Ordinary.[2] In the case of personal faculties granted by the Holy See, they expire with the person. Canon 61 implies practically the same for personal faculties granted by the Ordinaries.

If faculties are granted for a certain case or number of cases they expire after the application as stated or implied in the grant, or upon the cessation of the *causa finalis* that motived the concession. Likewise, if a time limit is set to the exercise of faculties, for instance *ad quinquennium,* they cease *lapsu temporis.*[3] Faculties granted for the internal forum are an exception. Canon 207, par. 2, legislates: *Sed potestate pro foro interno concessa, actus per inadvertentiam positus, elapso tempore vel exhausto casuum numero, validus est.*

The cessation of faculties by renunciation is unusual. In certain instances it would be disrespectful to the grantor and, most probably, disadvantageous or even harmful for the many who could benefit by the application of concessions.[4] The renunciation, to be effective would have to be accepted by a competent superior.

Revocation is as positive a cause of cessation as the granting is of the origin of faculties. To be effective, the revocation must be directly intimated to the possessor of faculties. (Cf. Can. 207, par. 1.) The extraordinary faculties, that had been granted to our bishops before the New Code, ceased in this manner.[5]

Faculties that have been *communicated*[6] do not cease by the mere fact that they have been revoked from the possession of the *communicans,* since the one to whom the faculties have been communicated possesses them in his own name.[7] A general revocation, however, would affect, by its very nature, also the communicated faculties. Delegated or sub-delegated faculties follow, as to cessation, the norm laid down in canon 207.

## Notes (Chapter VI)

1. Klekotka, *Diocesan Consultors,* pp. 163, sqq., Philadelphia, 1920.
2. Cf. D'Annibale, *op. cit.,* I, p. 216, footnote 26.
3. It is well worthy of mention that here in the United States recourse could be had to the Apostolic Delegate for a prorogation of the time limit of faculties granted by the Holy See. Art. 19 of Chapter I of his Excellency's faculties reads: *Prorogandi ad breve aliquod tempus facultates, indulgentias et indulta a S. Sede concessa, quae expiraverint quin tempestive postulatio pro eorum prorogatione ad S. Sedem missa fuerit, facta tamen obligatione statim recurrendi ad eamdem S. Sedem pro gratia aut (si petitio iam facta fuerit) pro responsione obtinenda.*
4. Cf. Canon 72.
5. *Proxima Sacra,* S. C. Cons. April 25, 1918: *Quapropter indulta quae hucusque, postulantibus Ordinariis, ad hunc finem* (Ecclesiae utilitatem et animarum salutem) *concedebantur, quaeque vel in Brevi dicto 25 annorum vel in formulis typis impressis ad decennium, ad quinquennium aut etiam ad triennium valituris continentur, supervacanea evadere videntur; . . . Ssmus D. N. Benedictus XV, . . . hoc S. C. Consistorialis decreto ea quae sequuntur statuit et sanxit:* (1) *exceptis locis S. Congregationi de Propaganda Fide subiectis . . . in universis scilicet dioecesibus iuri communi obnoxiis, facultates omnes pro foro externo Ordinariis concessae, quaeque n Formulis et Brevi superius recensitis continentur, a die* 18 *maii huius anni cessabunt, neque amplius in usu esse poterunt.*
6. Cf. Form. I, art. XXVIII, Form. C, art. X.
7. Putzer, *op. cit.,* p. 42.

# SECOND PART

## Diocesan Faculties

I

# FACULTAS ADMINISTRANDI OMNIA SACRAMENTA, CONFIRMATIONE ET ORDINE EXCEPTIS

The appointment to the *cura animarum* contains by its very nature not only the permission but also the obligation to administer the sacraments. The above-stated faculty is an explicit expression of the permission contained in the appointment. The faculty serves also as a *general summary* of the power the appointed or delegated priest has in regard to the ministration of the sacraments. The document of diocesan faculties contains other grants that concede certain *specific* powers for the administration of the various sacraments.

Though the faculty does not contain any modifying phrase or clause, it is understood that the permission granted in the faculty is to be used only according to the laws of the Church that govern the ministration of the sacraments. It is presupposed that the liturgical and canonical regulations prescribed by the Church in the matter of the sacraments are regarded as obligatory conditions for the proper exercise of the faculty here under consideration. A phrase, such as *servatis servandis,* would express the obviously implied obligation of observing the pertinent ecclesiastical laws in the use of this general faculty.

A general precept that can be considered as being of both liturgical and canonical import is contained in canon 731, par. 1: *Cum omnia Sacramenta Novae Legis, a Christo Domino Nostro instituta, sint praecipua sanctificationis et salutis media, summa in iis opportune riteque administrandis ac suscipiendis dilgientia et reverentia adhibenda est.*

Concerning the *liturgical* regulations the Code lays down the following law: *In Sacramentis conficiendis, administrandis ac suscipiendis accurate serventur ritus et caeremoiae quae in libris ritualibus ab Ecclesia probatis praecipiuntur.*[1] It is likewise prescribed that everyone follow his own rite, *salvo praescripto can. 851, par. 2, 866.*[2] Canon 851, par. 2, permits, under certain conditions (*ubi necessitas urgeat nec sacerdos diversi ritus adsit*), the distribution of Holy Communion *in fermentato* or *in azymo,* respectively. Canon 866 makes several concessions concerning rite in the matter of receiving Holy Communion.[3] Several other prescripts of a liturgical nature are stated in the general introductory canons of the Code on the Sacraments. They refer to the *benedictio* and *asservatio* of the Holy Oils.[4]

In the introductory canons on the Sacraments, the Code likewise establishes certain general *canonical* regulations for the ministration of the Sacraments. Canon 731, par. 1, forbids the ministration of the Sacraments to heretics or schismatics, even though they be in good faith until they have been reconciled with the Church.[5] This prohibitory law does not silence the opinion of theologians that conditional absolution may be granted to heretics and schismatics—even though they have been and are formally such—who are unconscious and at the point of death.[6] Capello[7] holds that, notwithstanding the present prohibitory law, a *material* heretic or schismatic, at the point of death, may be absolved conditionally, even though he is not unconscious.[8] *Salvo meliori iudicio,* these favorable opinions could be used in the ministration of Extreme Unction. Canon 732 forbids the *iteratio* of baptism, confirmation and Holy Orders and provides for the conditional *iteratio* in case of a prudent doubt. The last introductory canon (can. 736) forbids the minister to exact or even ask, directly or indirectly, *quavis de causa vel occasione* any offerings except those provided for in canon 1507, par. 1.

Particular canonical regulations to be observed in the administration of the Sacraments are established in the respective Titles dealing with the legislation on the Sacraments.

The phrase of the faculty *"Confirmatione et Ordine exceptis"* is usually added in the Faculty as a juridical finesse to the term *"omnia."*

## Notes

### Diocesan Faculties

#### I

1. Can. 733, par. 1.
2. Ibid. par. 2.
3. Can. 733, 2 does not refer to canon 905: *Cuivis fideli integrum est confessario legitime approbato etiam alius ritus, cui maluerit, peccata sua confiteri.*
4. Canons, 734, 735.
5. Can. 731, par. 2: *Vetitum est Sacramenta Ecclesiae ministare haereticis aut schismaticis, etiam bona fide errantibus eaque petentibus, nisi prius, erroribus reiectis, Ecclesiae reconciliati fuerint.*
6. Arregui, *Summarium Theol. Mor.*, p. 384; Capello, *De Sacramentis*, I, p. 53.
7. *Op. cit.*, p. 54.
8. Arregui, *op. cit.*, p. 384; aliique ibid.

## II

## FACULTAS ADHIBENDI IN BAPTISMO ADULTORUM, EX CAUSIS IN IURE DIOECESANO STATUTIS, CAEREMONIAS PRAESCRIPTAS PRO BAPTISMO INFANTIUM.

The Code permits the local Ordinary to grant the concession of baptizing grown up persons according to the ceremonies prescribed for the baptism of infants. To grant this concession, he must have a grave and reasonable cause.[1] The decision as to the value of the cause or causes rests with the Ordinary. The causes which the Ordinary considers grave and reasonable could be conveniently stated in the document of diocesan faculties, or, preferably, in the above-mentioned faculty itself. Blat[2] adds the following remark to "*rationabili de causa indulgere*": "*pro uno vel pluribus casibus vel ad tempus particulariter.*" This restriction, suggested, perhaps, by the tenor of the canon, would limit the power of the Ordinary as to the time extension of the faculty. There is no evident objection to establishing a permanent faculty on the canon in question.

The Code[3] defines the terms "infant" and "adult" as follows: *Cum agitur de baptismo*: 1) *Parvulorum seu infantium nomine veniunt, ad normam can.* 88, *par.* 3, *qui nondum rationis usum adepti sunt, eisdemque accensentur amentes ab infantia, in quavis aetate constituti*: 2) *Adulti autem censentur, qui rationis usu fruuntur.*[4]

*Salvo meliori iudicio,* it would not be permissible to use the *formula infantium* in place of the *formula adultorum* on the basis that *custom* has juridically established such a right. The S. Cong. Rituum gave a negative reply to the following question: *An inveterata quaecumque in contrarium* (concerning a rubric or decree on a procession with the Blessed Sacrament) *consuetudo derogare possit legi a Decretis Sacrae Congregationis praescriptae?* Wapelhorst[5] writes: *Consuetudines, etsi immemorabiles, quae Rubricis vel Decretis S. Rit. Congregationis aperte repugnant, sustineri nequeunt.*

The Ordinary could add, to the faculty under consideration, the permission to baptize, *privately,* grown up heretics who are to be baptized conditionally.[6] Private baptism is defined in canon 737, par. 2: *Cum ministratur* (*scl. baptismus*) *servatis omnibus ritibus et caeremoniis quae in ritualibus libris praecipiuntur, appellatur sollemnis; secus, non sollemnis seu privatus.* Strictly speaking, all prayers, formulas and ceremonies could be dropped except the actual ceremony of baptism itself in conferring private baptism.[7] Apparently no special reason is required for granting this permission, as there is for the former concession.

## Notes

### II

1. Canon 755, par. 2: *Loci Ordinarius potest gravi et rationabili de causa indulgere ut caeremoniae praescriptae pro baptismo infantium adhibeantur in baptismo adultorum.*
2. Comment, Text. Iur. Can. III, pars. I, page 48.
3. Can. 745, par. 2.
4. An indult, dated Feb. 6, 1859, granted the bishops of the province of St. Louis the right to use the ceremonies prescribed for the baptism of infants when baptizing adults. The request for this indult was couched in the following terms: . . . *ut in baptismo adultorum liceat uti formula in baptismo parvulorum adhibenda usque dum S. Sedes aliter statuerit.* The reply granted the request, but added: *interim curent* (*scl. Ordinarii*) *de inducenda formula pro adultis a Rituali Romano praescripta.*
5. *Compendium S. Liturgiae,* ed. 6, 1904, n. 5.
6. Can. 759, par. 2: *Extra mortis periculum baptismum privatum loci Ordinarius permittere nequit, nisi agatur de haereticis qui in adulta aetate sub conditione baptizentur.*
7. Blat, *Comment. Text. Iur. Can.* III, ed. 1920, page 24.

## III

## FACULTAS CELEBRANDI MISSAM

The general *permission* to celebrate mass is one of the usual faculties granted by the Ordinary to priests under his charge. In a certain sense *this faculty is not so much a permission to celebrate mass as it is a testimonial* that the priest who wishes to use it is a clergyman in good standing in the diocese or the religious institute. Canon 805 *obliges* all priests to offer up the Holy Sacrifice several times a year, and imposes upon bishops and religious superiors the duty of seeing to it that the priests under their jurisdiction say mass at least on Sundays and feast days of obligation.

There is no prescript in the Code that obliges a priest first to obtain permission to say mass. The Ordinary may of course prescribe certain norms or rules that are to be followed in admitting priests to the celebration of mass, and there are, no doubt, good reasons why in certain places very strict rules are laid down in this matter. An investigation of the Code legislation on the permission to say mass will be of some value in clearing up various points that are both of theoretical and practical import.

### The "Celebret"

Canon 804 enters into the details and conditions of the procedure to be followed in granting a *"sacerdos extraneus"* the permission to celebrate mass. It is to be noted at the very outset of this consideration that the canon uses a term that does not refer to extra-diocesan priests only, but includes all priests who are not connected with that church for which the permission to celebrate is asked. The term is: *sacerdos extraneus ecclesiae in qua celebrare postulat.* Every priest provided with the required testimonial letters is to be admitted to the celebration of mass. As to the number of times such a priest is to be admitted, no direction is given in the Code. Unless an authoritative interpretation is placed on the words of the canon that would limit the number of times or require the approval of the local ordinary after a certain number of times, there seems to be no reason why the rector of the church should limit the extent of the permission granted by the Code. Indeed, the terms of the canon, at their face value, do not give the Ordinary the power of limiting the permissions to say mass, provided, of course, the priest is in possession of the required testimonials. For we read in the third paragraph of this canon: *Peculiares hac de re normae, salvis huius canonis praescriptis, ab Ordinario loci datae, servandae sunt ab omnibus, etc.* A regulation that would forbid a priest in possession of the proper testimonials to say mass or that would place prohibitive restrictions upon the grant made by the Code would fail against *"salvis huius canonis praescriptis."* Though a priest be in possession of the required testimonials, he is not to be admitted to the celebration of mass if it is certain that he has committed an act that would suffice to deny him the permission. In other words even though his testimonials are authentic and, as far as the time limit is concerned, are still valid, the permission is to be withheld, if he has done anything that would justify the denial.

What would constitute a sufficient cause of refusal is set forth in various parts of the Code. It is important to note, however, before considering the grounds of refusal, the terms the Code uses in canon 804, par. 1: *nisi interim aliquid eum commisisse constet, cur a Missae celebratione repelli debeat.* These terms indicate that the time limit given in the testimonials is not to be considered as of further value, that the testimonials are not to be accepted as *adhuc validae,* once the petitioner has made himself guilty of a *delictum* excluding him from the use of his testimonials.

The *litterae commendatitiae* lose their commendatory force as far as the celebration of mass is concerned if the bearer has incurred an excommunication,[1] a personal interdict,[2] or a suspension that forbids the celebration of mass.[3] Any act, sufficiently known, of a defamatory or scandalous nature would come under the heading of reasons *"cur a Missae celebratione repelli debeat"* (*scl. "sacerdos extraneus"*).

The permission is to be denied only when it is *certain* that the petitioner (*sacerdos extraneus*) is guilty of an act invalidating his testimonial letters as to his admissibility to the celebration of mass. Hence, doubtful or unsubstantiated reports, suspicions or unreliable statements about the conduct or attitude of the petitioning priest are by no means sufficient reasons to keep him from celebrating mass. If the legislator had wished to include the cases just mentioned, he no doubt would have used terms broad enough to cover them. A term similar to *prudenter dubitatur* would have covered more cases than are included in *"constat,"* but, at the same time, would not have done justice to the consideration that the number of undeserving clerics is a relatively negligible quantity.

The present legislation concerning admission to the celebration of mass is couched in positive terms, whereas the law of pre-Code times bore a negative stamp. Our present law reads as follows: *Sacerdos extraneus . . . exhibens litteras—commendatitias—admittatur.* Canon 7 Dist. LXXI in the *Decretum Gratianum* sounds rather prohibitive: *Extraneo clerico . . . extra civitatem suam sine commendatitiis litteris proprii episcopi nusquam penitus liceat celebrare. "Nullus clericus"* in the words of the Council of Trent[4] *"peregrinus sine commendatitiis sui Ordinarii litteris ab ullo episcopo ad divina celebranda et sacramenta administranda admittatur."* The *Litterae Encyclicae* of the S. Cong. de Prop. Fide, April 20, 1873, are likewise of a negative cast. The pre-Code legislation did not consider the positive case in which a priest possesses the required testimonials, and hence did not express its mind on the nature of the admission to the celebration of mass in such a case, namely, as to whether the petitioning priest could or should or must be allowed to say mass. Apparently this point was left to the local Ordinaries for further regulation, where such supervision was at all required by circumstances. It is not improbable that the former legislation took for granted that a priest in possession of the proper letters would undoubtedly be admitted to the celebration of mass. The negative legislation of pre-Code times finds its substance, modified by considerable leniency, in the second paragraph of canon 804 of the Code.

The term *admittatur* deserves careful consideration, since it seems to have been chosen with much precision. In the first place, it is worth noticing that *admittatur* was chosen in preference to *admitti potest.* This choice does not leave the admission of a strange priest in good standing to the discretion or discrimination of the rector of the church. The *admitti potest* is substantially and sufficiently contained in the authentic and valid testimonial letters of the visitor's legitimate ecclesiastical superior. That superior has by his letters settled the question as to whether the priest desiring to celebrate mass can be admitted. The *admittatur* inculcates respect for the authentic and valid *"litterae commendatitiae"* of any and every Ordinary who issues them. On the other hand, the term *admitti debet* has been carefully avoided so as not to state, perhaps, an obligation, imposed upon the rector of the church, that would outweigh the consideration of possibly disagreeable circumstances connected with the granting of the "request" of the visiting priest. The term *"admittatur"* cannot be said to contain a strict obligation, but it does constitute a mild obligation, which, *positively considered,* is binding until it comes in contact with overruling circumstances of time, trouble and expense for the rector of the church or the church itself. *Negatively considered,* the obligation is such that aside from the circumstances just mentioned no local or territorial legislation can be effective against the admission legislated by the Code. Local or territorial legislation could, and in instances does, require *plenissimo iure* that the *"litterae commendatitiae"* be submitted to the Curia for examination. But if the letters are authentic and valid according to canon 804, par. 1, no particular legislation or decision can *per se* obstruct the admission.[5]

In connection with the *facultas celebrandi,* implied by the testimonial letters, the question immediately arises as to what is meant by the term: *"authenticae et adhuc validae litterae commendatitiae."* The *authenticity* of the letters can be established by the signature or the seal or some other means whereby the objective authority is recognizable, such as, *"consideratis considerandis,"* an accompanying picture of the episcopal coat of arms, the wording of the letterhead, the official form of the letter, provided, of course, that these indications are confirmed by collateral proofs. The testimonials are, moreover, to be *"adhuc validae."* This term has reference primarily to the time limit up to which the letters are to remain in force. The term could refer also to the fulfillment of a condition, as for instance, the wearing of the clerical garb. The time limit depends, of course, upon the superior who grants the letter. Various elements of a laudatory, corrective, physical (health), or other nature may be of decisive influence with the superior in placing a time limit upon the force of the letters. A time limit dependent upon the fulfillment or non-fulfillment of a certain condition need not, as is worthy of pointing out, be construed as in any way derogatory to the character of the visitor nor as ill-fitting with the concept of "commendatory" letter. The wording of the condition might be taken verbatim from ecclesiastical legislation, general or particular, as for instance: "*dummodo ecclesiastica veste indutus, etc.,*" terms taken from can. 804, par. 2.

What are the "*litterae commendatitiae*"? Gasparri answers that they are those letters whereby "*Ordinarius testatur de legitima ordinatione, de carentia cuiuslibet censurae et irregularitatis, de bonis moribus ipsius clerici, eumque alieno episcopo commendat.*"[6] This definition contains four elements: (1) a certificate of ordination, (2) negatively, the absence of censures and irregularities, (3) positively, the good standing, (4) the actual commendation. The explicit certification of the bearer's ordination is, of course, not necessary, if the superior implies that fact in the course, or by the purpose, of the letter. However, attestation to the fact of ordination is more in keeping with the official nature of the testimonials. The absence of censures and irregularities seems worthy of mention in a document that purposes to put aside all doubt concerning the admissibility of the bearer to the celebration of mass, which admissibility is obstructed chiefly by censures and irregularities. The testimonial "*de bonis moribus*" is highly desirable, though not necessary, and sometimes not applicable, as in the case of a cleric who has just been absolved from censures. While it would be very appropriate to permit such a priest to celebrate mass for reasons of spiritual benefits, it would hardly be commensurate with the objective truth to commend him because of "good standing." The *formal commendation* is a most welcome feature in any testimonial, and especially, in one that speaks for admission to the celebration of mass.

According to the terms of the Code in canon 804, par. 1, the legislation is concerned with the "*litterae commendatitiae*" of priests only. No mention whatsoever is made of the requirements for the admission of a bishop to the celebration of mass. The case in which a travelling bishop, unknown to the rector of the church and without authentic indications of his office, requesting admission to celebrate mass, is exceptionally rare, and is well provided for in the second paragraph of canon 804, if any timidly conscientious interpreter of the law would classify bishops among those meant by the Code as "*sacerdotes extranei.*"

The usual name given the *litterae commendatitiae* is *Celebret.* This term may have found its origin in some ordinary formula, or it may have been taken from the purpose for which the letter of commendation was written. The principal purpose of the *litterae commendatitiae* is the admission of the bearer to the celebration of mass. The terms of the Code, however, do not indicate that this purpose is to be their exclusive object, nor are they customarily understood to be issued for that sole purpose. The *litterae commendatitiae* are frequently a means of obtaining all the faculties of the diocese.

The term *commendatitiae* seems to imply that the letters are to be specifically formulated. In other words, the ordinary pamphlet of the diocesan faculties would not suffice *per se.* If, however, the pamphlet contains a commendatory statement concerning the grantee, there seems to be no reason why the grant of faculties could not be accepted as commendatory, at least within the confines of the diocese where the faculties are granted. It would mean stretching a point of the law to claim that such a commendation should receive, outside the diocese, full recognition as meant by the Code in "*admittatur,*" since the faculties might be granted to some priest whom the Ordinary desires to retain for peculiar reasons within the diocese.

The testimonial letters are to be given by the Ordinaries ("*sui Ordinarii*") for secular priests, by Religious Superiors for religious, and by the Sacred Congregation for the Oriental Church for priests of an oriental rite.[7]

The Code has legislated quite explicitly for the case when the "*sacerdos extraneus*" has *no commendatory letters.* The rector of the church may permit him to say mass *"si de eius (scl. sacerdotis extranei) probitate apprime constet."* Hence, there is *no obligation* by law to admit any priest, no matter how well his good standing is certified, if the proper letters are lacking.

If the visitor is unknown to the rector and is without the *"litterae commendatitiae,"* he *may be permitted* to say mass once or twice, provided certain conditions are verified. The first condition is the minimum that can be required in the nature of an indication pointing to the clerical state, namely: the wearing of the ecclesiastical garb. Though the wearing of the garb is no convincing proof, the absence of it in the case of an unknown visitor is surely a cause for doubt. The Code does not demand that the visitor appear in the ecclesiastical garb of the region where he happens to be sojourning, but simply states *"ecclesiastica veste indutus."* This is well worth remembering, since priests hailing from foreign countries are not always dressed in the clerical garb of this country.

The second condition is that the visitor receive nothing by reason of the celebration of mass from the church, in which he says mass, upon any title whatsoever, *"quovis titulo."* This does not mean, however, that this condition would be invalidated if the rector of the church were to give the visitor a stipend of his own purse for one of the parish masses.

The third condition is that the stranger write his name, office and diocese in a special book. The purpose of this condition is to obtain some kind of tangible evidence for later reference, and to make it impossible or, at least more difficult, for an imposter to continue for a considerable length of time in his work of fraud. The special book mentioned in this third condition is not listed among the *"libri paroeciales"* in canon 470, par. 1. The parish priest is not obliged by the Code to send in to the episcopal Curia an *"authenticum exemplar"* of this special book, though this obligation may be imposed, of course, by diocesan statute or episcopal regulation.

The detailed legislation, we have just considered, is new as far as general law is concerned. In fact, the pre-Code law concerning *clerici peregrini* excluded strictly any priest from admission to the celebration of mass who was without the *litterae commendatitiae.* The Council of Trent decreed: *Nullus praeterea clericus peregrinus sine commendatitiis sui Ordinarii litteris ab ullo episcopo ad divinia celebranda et sacramenta administranda admittatur.*[8] This decree swept aside the exception which Innocent III had made in favor of those who asked to say mass *"secreto ex devotione."*[9] The term *clericus peregrinus* seems to have been tempered down to mean *"clericus vagus et ignotus.*[10]

The final paragraph of canon 804 treats of the particular regulations given by the Ordinaries concerning the admission of *"sacerdotes extranei"* to the celebration of mass. As stated above, the regulations of the Ordinary are not to conflict with the general law laid down in canon 804: *"Salvis huius canonis praescriptis."* In the opinion of Gasparri[11] and Wernz[12] a priest in possession of the required testimonial letters cannot *per se* be refused admission to the celebration of mass.[13] The reason given is as follows: *"Sacerdos dispositus et nullo impedimento detentus, ex sua ordinatione habet ius ad Missae celebrationem, quam Ecclesia jubet aut suadet."*[14] The general law of the Church allows the rector of a church to grant a priest who is not in possession of the *litterae commendatitiae* permission to say mass, under the conditions mentioned above.[15] This concession to the rector of the church in which the *"sacerdos extraneus"* wishes to celebrate, is also comprehended under *"salvis huius canonis praescriptis,"* unless an unwarranted interpretation were to take *"praescripta"* in a most literal sense, which interpretation would not agree with the

Code's use of this term. The Code does not explicitly state in so many words that this concession is made to the rector of the church, but such seems to be the obvious interpretation deducible especially from the second part of paragraph 2 of the canon here under consideration.

Whatever regulations are made in this matter by the Ordinary of the place, they are to be observed by all, including the exempt religious, unless when the latter wish to say mass in churches of their own religious institute. As is evident from the wording of the law, exempt religious are obliged to observe the particular regulations of the Ordinary of the place if it is question of permitting a secular or a non-exempt religious priest to celebrate mass in a church of a religious institute. The law states expressly that the regulations are not obligatory for religious of an exempt institute if they are to say mass in a church of *their own* religious institute. Hence, if an exempt religious desires to say mass in a church of an exempt religious institute to which he does not belong, the regulations of the Ordinary of the place are to be observed.

By way of an appendix to the remarks on the obligation of the rector of a church to admit an "*extraneus sacerdos*" to the celebration of the Sacrifice and in connection with the preceding paragraph on the particular regulations of the Ordinary in this matter, it might be useful to adduce a regulation of the Code concerning the expenses on occasion of the services here under consideration. Canon 1303, par. 2, legislates as follows: "*Si qua ecclesia paupertate laboret, potest Ordinarius permittere ut a sacerdotibus qui in proprium commodum inibi celebrent, propter utensilia ceteraque ad Missae sacrificium necessaria, moderata stipes exigatur.* This provision would, no doubt, be of great advantage to some poor church situated near a railroad station or steamship dock. Travelling priests would gladly pay the "*taxa utensilium*" to avoid the delay in going to a church further away. The rector must have the permission therefore of the Ordinary to exact the "*taxa.*" As the canon states in the third paragraph, it pertains to the bishop, and not to the Vicar Capitular or the Vicar General "*sine speciali mandato*" to decide the amount of the moderate tax; and no person is allowed to demand a higher sum. Exempt religious, also, must observe this decree of the bishop. And the final paragraph of the same canon legislates that such a decree given for the whole diocese, should be made by the bishop in the diocesan synod, if possible. If the decree is given outside the synod, the Chapter, or the council of diocesan consultors, is first to be heard on the matter. Cappello[16] adds that to demand an amount higher than that stated by the decree is a sin against justice and makes the offender subject to the obligation of restitution. If this opinion is to be accepted, a distinction should be made between the case in which the rector of the church is obliged to admit the "*sacerdos extraneus*" and the case in which he is not obliged to do so. In the former, the injustice would be more apparent because the visitor has a right that should not be obstructed.

## Notes

### III

1. Can. 2261.
2. Can. 2275.
3. Can. 2279.
4. *Sess.* XXIII, cap. 16.
5. Cappello, *De Sacramentis*, I, p. 600: *Normae ab Ordinario loci datae, quae opponantur praescriptis cit. canonis* (804), *sunt ipso iure nullae ac irritae.*
6. *Op. cit.*, I, page 259.
7. Can. 804, par. 1.
8. Sess. XXIII, cap. 16, *de reform.*
9. C. 3, X, *de clericis peregrinis*, I, 22.
10. Gasparri, *De Sanctissima Eucharistia* I, pag 261.
11. *Op. cit.*, I, page 265, sq.
12. *Op. cit.*, III, 2, page 166, footnote 51.
13. Cf. Cappello, *op. cit.*, I, p. 600.
14. Gasparri, *op. cit.*, *loc. cit.*
15. Cf. canon 804, par. 2.
16. *Op. cit.*, I, page 602.

## IV

## FACULTAS CELEBRANDI BIS IN DIEBUS DOMINICIS ET FESTIS DE PRAECEPTO, SI NOTABILIS FIDELIUM PARS MISSAE ADSTARE NON POSSIT

The faculty for binating and for celebrating mass under conditions forbidden by general law was formerly given to our bishops under article XXIII of Formula I and was worded in the following terms: *Celebrandi bis in die, si necessitas urgeat, ita tamen ut in prima Missa non sumpserit ablutionem,—per unam horam ante auroram et aliam post meridiem,—sine ministro,—et sub dio et sub terra, in loco tamen decenti,—etiamsi altare sit fractum vel sine reliquiis sanctorum,—et praesentibus haereticis, schismaticis, infidelibus et excommunicatis,—si aliter celebrari non possit. Caveat vero, ne praedicta facultate seu dispensatione celebrandi bis in die aliter quam ex gravissimis causis et rarissime utatur, in quo graviter ipsius conscientia oneratur. Quod si hanc eamdem facultatem alteri Sacerdoti iuxta potestatem inferius apponendam communicare, aut causas utendi alicui, qui a Sancta Sede hanc facultatem obtinuerit, approbare visum fuerit, serio ipsius conscientiae injungitur, ut paucis dumtaxat, iisque maturioris prudentiae ac zeli et qui absolute necessarii sunt, nec pro quolibet loco, sed ubi gravis necessitas tulerit, et ad breve tempus eamdem communicet aut respective causas approbet.*

The various elements: bination, time, place and so forth, that enter into this faculty are treated in several canons of the New Code and in some points have been subjected to legislational changes.

## Canon 806

The matter of bination, or more precisely of celebrating more than one mass a day is treated succinctly and definitely in canon 806. This canon legislates:

(1) *Excepto die Nativitatis Domini et die Commemorationis omnium fidelium defunctorum, quibus facultas est ter offerendi Eucharisticum Sacrificum, non licet sacerdoti plures in die celebrare Missas, nisi ex apostolico indulto aut potestate facta a loci Ordinario.*

(2) *Hanc tamen facultatem impertiri nequit Ordinarius, nisi cum, prudenti ipsius iudicio, propter penuriam sacerdotum die festo de praecepto notabilis fidelium pars Missae adstare non possit; non est autem in eius potestate plures quam duas Missas eidem sacerdoti permittere.*

The first part of the canon which refers to the faculty of saying three masses on the Feast of the Nativity of the Lord and on All Souls' Day is beyond the scope of our inquiry in these pages. We should like to call attention, however, to the use of the term "faculty" in this canon. "Faculty" is used here obviously in the sense of permission, both in the first and in the second paragraph of the canon. A glance at the wording of the canon shows that "*facultas,*" "*permittere,*" "*potestas*" and "*licet*" are used synonymously.

The general law concerning the number of times mass may be celebrated is summed up in the words: *non licet sacerdoti plures in die celebrare Missas, nisi ex apostolico indulto aut potestate facta a loci Ordinario.*

The earliest trace of a law forbidding the repeated celebration of Mass is to be found in the Decree of Gratian, c. 53, Dist. I, *de cons.* The law itself is not couched in terms that directly forbid the celebration of more than one mass a day by the same priest, but the intention of the legislator, Alexander II (1061-1073), is plainly discernible: *Sufficit sacerdoti unam in die celebrare missam, quia Christus semel passus est, et totum mundum redemit. Non modica res est unam missam facere, et valde felix qui unam digne celebrare potest. Quidam tamen pro defunctis unam faciunt, et alteram de die, si necesse sit. Qui vero pro pecuniis aut adulationibus secularium una die presumunt plures facere missas, non estimo, evadere damnationem.*

Innocent III expressed the prohibition in the same terms: *Consuluisti nos, utrum presbyter duas missas in eadem die valeat celebrare; super quo tibi Respondemus, quod, excepto die Nativitatis dominicae, nisi causa necessitatis suadeat, sufficit sacerdoti semel in die unam missam solummodo celebrare.*[1]

Honorius III interpreted the term *sacerdos* as comprehending also members of the hierarchy: *Quum . . . cuilibet sacerdoti, quacunque dignitate praefulgeat, unam in die celebrare missam sufficiat.*[2] The mandate in which this interpretation occurs was given in reply to an inquiry from the "*Archiepiscopus Sipontinus.*"

We find in this and in subsequent legislation that by common law the priest was permitted to say more than one mass in cases of necessity (*nisi causa necessitatis suadeat*). Benedict XIV (*Declarasti Nobis,* March 16, 1746) writes: *Certissimum illud est missionariis tantum a Sede Apostolica potestatem aliquando fieri, ut uno die Sacrificium bis operentur; reliquis vero sacerdotibus opus esse, ut hac de re facultatem ab episcopo consequantur, etiamsi causa necessitatis intercedere videatur; cuius sane iudicium ad ipsos sacerdotes nequaquam pertinet.* The permission was at all events to be used dependently upon the decision of the bishop.

The foregoing quotation from *Declarasti Nobis* seems to imply that the faculty itself was not granted by common law. However, the paragraph from which the quotation is taken, considered in its entirety, primarily stresses the condition of necessity, and is not concerned with the source of the faculty as such. That point had been settled in previous parts of the same letter. The *Instructio* S. C. de Prof. Fide, 24 May, 1870, likewise teaches that the faculty of saying more than one mass a day is granted by common law, but that it is to be exercised *"dependenter ab Ordinario."* The pertinent passage reads: *In his casibus iterari Missa potest etiam ab iis, qui facultate non sunt donati per Formulas, quae concedi solent per S. Congregationem Fidei propagandae praepositam, cum id concedat ipsum commune ius, semper tamen dependenter ab Ordinario, ad quem pertinet tum de vera necessitate, tum de possibilitate canonica remedia applicandi, ferre sententiam.*

The *Instructio* quotes Benedict XIV expressly on the two points just mentioned: *Quae huc usque dicta sunt, canonicis etiam generalibus sanctionibus innituntur.*

The New Code divides canon 806 into two paragraphs. The first deals with the faculty, as such, of saying more than one mass a day, the second deals with the limitations of the Ordinary's power in granting the faculty.

The New Code has withdrawn the concession which formerly common law granted for cases of necessity. The faculty, as such, must henceforth come from the Ordinary or from the Apostolic See. All the general sanctions, in so far as they granted the *"facultas iterandi missam eodem die"* in cases of necessity are abrogated, or better said, are corrected to a stricter view. Now both the faculty and the judgment as to the required conditions are matters under the jurisdiction of the Ordinary.

Before taking up a discussion of this legislational change we should consider the fact that although common law granted the faculty upon the consent of the Ordinary, the faculty was nevertheless expressly granted by particular law, e. g. in various Formulas. The faculty of binating granted by the Holy See to Ordinaries in mission countries would have been superfluous if it contained nothing beyond the power granted by common law. Thus states the *Instructio,* after bringing forward the cases of necessity in which according to common law the priest could, upon consent of the Ordinary, celebrate more than one mass a day.

The cases are those adduced by Benedict XIV in his constitution *Declarasti Nobis.* According to the unanimous opinion of theologians the celebration of more than one mass a day was permissible for a priest *"qui duas parochias obtineat, vel duos populos adeo seiunctos, ut alter ipsorum parocho celebranti per dies festos adesse nullo modo possit ob locorum maximam distantiam."* The other case is as follows: *"Quando una tantum sit ecclesia, in qua Missa celebratur, et ad quam insimul universus populus convenire non potest."*

The faculty granted by particular law comprehended, therefore, according to the *Instructio* other cases of necessity not mentioned in the common law. The faculty served, moreover, to settle the disquieting doubts that harassed the missionary bishops and priests. The faculty, superadded to the faculty granted by common law, was not superfluous, therefore, because of these two reasons: *objectively* it was applicable in a larger number of cases; *subjectively* it served as a reassurance to the doubting and timid conscience.[3]

For us in this country, who have been accustomed heretofore to obtaining the faculty of binating from the bishop, who in turn received the faculty in the Formulas, the legislational change is of no further serious practical import. One purpose of the superadded faculty was to cover cases that had found no place in common law. These cases are well provided for in the new legislation.

The tendency of the Code on this point is towards a stricter interpretation of the faculty of binating. The present wording of the law may be taken as an indication of the tendency toward a stricter interpretation. Although formerly the concession granted by common law to the ordinary priest was practically annulled by its dependence on the decision of the Ordinary, still theoretically considered, the concession granted directly to the priest remained more, perhaps, as a reminder to him of his obligation towards the people entrusted to his care, than as a grant of power. Benedict XIV insinuates this when speaking of a pastor in charge of two parishes: *Parochum nedum posse, sed plane teneri bis eodem die Missam celebrare.*[4]

The wording of the New Code takes away from the priest whatever grant of power as to binating was contained in the terminology of the old law, and also whatever responsibility went with its interpretation. The Ordinary is now by common law the one source both of the faculty and of the decision as to its applicability.[5] Whatever weight of obligation, according to the "*concors opinio theologorum,*" arises from being in charge of two parishes, that responsibility rests now primarily with the Ordinary. It is to him that the law now refers completely the matter of bination faculties. The New Code has therewith insinuated that bination is a matter to be considered more gravely than the old law indicated.[6]

Before taking up the second paragraph of can. 806 we must note that the law reads: "*non licet sacerdoti plures in die celebrare Missas, nisi ex apostolico indulto aut potestate facta a loci Ordinario.*" In 1879 and 1896 the Sacred Congregation of the Council granted the indult of *trination.*[7] Avanzini in his commentary on the *Acta Sanctae Sedis*[8] taught that in cases of necessity a priest could celebrate three or four masses. At the time of this commentary there was no apparently solid reason to the contrary. However, in 1893 a decree of the Sacred Congregation of the Council (in S. Josephi de Costarica, 6 May, 1893) forbade a third mass on the same day by the same priest "*quocumque in casu.*"[9] Gasparri answers the question why a priest in charge of three parishes is forbidden to say three masses with the reason that the proper parochial care of three parishes on the same day, namely, ministration of the sacraments and preaching, over and above the celebration of mass, is morally impossible.[10] It is not improbable that this normal impossibility gave rise to a custom which exempted pastors from the obligation of attending to more than two charges on the same day, and in the course of time forbade a third mass because of the moral impossibility of giving each flock the proper care. Theoretically considered, the same reason that would oblige a pastor to say mass on Sundays and Holy Days of obligation for two parishes would likewise make him responsible for the same duty in three or four parishes.[11]

The faculty of trinating is granted by common law for the Feast of Christmas and the Commemoration of All Souls. Mention of the custom of saying three masses on Christmas is found in St. Gregory's homily on the gospel of St. Luke.[12] Innocent III[13] considers Christmas an exception to the general rule, according to which only one mass a day is permissible, but he does not state how many masses are allowed on Christmas itself. The occidental custom of trinating on Christmas never found its way into the Oriental Church. Since the very first canon of the New Code limits the new legislation to the Latin Church—*exceptis excipiendis*—the privilege of trinating on Christmas and All Souls' Day is not extended to the Oriental Church. The concession of trinating on All Soul's Day granted by Benedict XIV to priests in Spain and its possession in 1748[14], was extended by Benedict XV[15] to the whole Latin Church.

In considering the exercise of the faculty of binating it is presupposed that no other priest is available for the celebration of the second mass, for if another priest is present who can and may say mass the faculty of binating does not hold. Such has always been the interpretation of the law and the New Code treats this point at least in a general way in the phrase "*propter penuriam sacerdotum.*"

Relatively to this expression, the question could be raised as to whether a priest, deprived of the privilege of saying mass, e. g. by suspension, could be called upon to celebrate the second mass. If we go back to the interpretation of the old law in this matter we shall find that the term "*valeat*" (*qui populi necessitati valeat satisfacere*) is equivalent to "*licite possit.*[16]

The obligation of using the services of another priest, if available, is undoubtedly a serious one. To lay down definite limits to this obligation is impossible. The whole matter should be left to the judgment of the Ordinary who will decide as to what is meant by the "*penuria sacerdotum*" mentioned in the second paragraph of can. 806. A general norm could be borrowed from the Third Plenary Council of Baltimore, no. 103: *Hucusque nulla praecisa regula voluit Ecclesia determinare quandonam alioquin legitima vel imo necessaria sit missae iteratio. Maluit potius rem decernendam relinquere judicio Ordinariorum ut in prudentia et charitate sua pro causae gravitate missam iterent vel a suis missionariis iterari permittant.* And no. 104 states: *Sed neque vult Sancta Sedes ut ob timorem rigoris quo munitur facultatis formula nimis angantur eadem utentes. E saepius enim repetitis Apostolicis declarationibus et responsis manifestum est ad iterationem veram quidem requiri necessitatem, haudquaquam tamen absolutam sed moralem, quae existere censenda est quoties deficiente presbyterorum copia aliisque omnibus circumstantiis mature perpensis judicetur, fidelibus vehementer utile fore ut sacerdotes bis missam eodem festo die celebrent. Cuiusmodi si adfuerit, non tantum haud timeant reatum illicitae iterationis, sed potius existiment se muneri suo defuturos, si vel ipsi pro populi necessitate missam non iteraverint vel missionariis suis hanc facultatem non concesserint.*

Visiting priests would have to be called upon to say one of the Sunday masses, but there is no evidence of an *obligation binding such priests* to accept. The Code contains nothing which could warrant the statement of such an obligation. It could be argued that if it is not permissible for a priest to binate if another priest is present who could say one of the masses, the obligation of the visiting priest is plainly implied. However, it is not at all evident that the "*penuria sacerdotum*" mentioned by the Code is alleviated by the presence of a visiting priest.[17]

The faculty of binating holds good only for Sundays and feast days of obligation. The latter are listed explicitly in can. 1247.

The fundamental motive for granting the faculty of binating is stated in the words of canon 806, par. 2: *cum . . . notabilis fidelium pars Missae adstare non possit.* The term "*notabilis*" permits of a certain latitude. The *Instructio* of 1870 goes into a brief discussion of the number of faithful sufficient to justify the granting of the faculty of bination. The decision, it states, is to be left to the charity and conscience of the Ordinary. Arregui holds that twenty people form a congregation large enough to permit bination.[18] The Sacred Congregation of the Council issued a rescript[19] in which bination was permitted for a parish consisting of about twenty persons. The faculty of bination for the benefit of fifteen or twenty persons was denied by the Sacred Congregation of the Inquisition.[20] The *Instructio* of 1870 seems to take it for granted that twenty persons would not constitute a sufficient number, although it admits that in peculiar cases, such as mentioned in a decree of October 5, 1688, of the Sacred Cong. de Prop. Fide, bination could be permitted for less than ten or fifteen persons.

The Code does not mention the causes from which the inability on the part of the parishioners to attend mass may arise. Formerly the two ordinary causes were, as quoted above, the following: (1) Two distinct parishes that could not attend the same mass because of the obstacle of distance; (2) a parish too large for the one parish-church. These two cases are undoubtedly covered by the New Code, for in both there is a *"notabilis pars"* that would miss mass if it were not for bination. A mild interpretation of the *"notabilis pars"* includes religious communities, hospitals and prison congregations. In such cases the *"pars"* is frequently more *"notabilis"* as a spiritual unit than as a physical number. It is patent that there is more reason for granting the faculty of bination for the benefit of strictly cloistered nuns than for other religious.

This brings us to the discussion of what the Code means by the term *"adstare non possit."* If we go back again to the cases mentioned in *Declarasi Nobis* and the *Instructio* of 1870 we find that as far as common law was concerned one indication of a norm for judging the impossibility of attending a mass of obligation was couched in the following terms: *ut alter (populus) ipsorum parocho celebrandi per dies festos adesse nullo modo possit ob locorum maximam distantiam.* This rather rigorous attitude is somewhat tempered in the particular law as explained in the *Instructio* of 1870, which sums up its explanatory commentary by quoting from a decree of the Sacred Cong. de Prop. Fide (not given in the Collectanea) of 1832 to the bishop of Nicopolis in Bulgaria: *Intelligendas (scl. clausulas Formularum) haud esse in extremo rigore, habito prae oculis principio, Sedem Apostolicam dictam facultatem concedere in bonum spirituale fidelium, desiderio, ut omnes praeceptum ecclesiasticum adimplere facile possint.* A concrete case of the wrong use of the faculty of bination is found mentioned in a reply of the Congregation of Holy Rites, May 22, 1841, to the question: *An liceat Parocho in urbe constituto iterare Missam iisdem diebus super diversa quidem Altaria, sed tantummodo ad consulendum parochianorum commoditati; v. gr. ut celebretur Missa hora octava, quando iam celebratur variis horis, videlicet hora sexta, septima, nona et decima?* The answer of the Congregation reads: *Sine speciali Apostolico Indulto non licere; et teneri Episcopum consuetudinem seu abusum omnino eliminare.*[21]

The two guiding causes in the former law, both common and particular, that permitted the use of the faculty of bination were "*necessitas populi*" and "*raritas sacerdotum.*" The principle of *accommodating* the parishioners with another mass was considered an "*abusus omnino eliminandus.*" The wording of the new legislation on bination precludes any interpretation that would permit the application of this principle.

The Code adds the definite legislation that it is beyond the power of the Ordinary to permit the same priest to celebrate more than two masses. The opinion of Avanzini, mentioned above, namely, that under given conditions a priest could celebrate three or four masses on days of obligation is thereby again declared untenable.[22]

The question whether the Ordinary himself is forbidden by Canon 806 to binate except in cases of necessity, is answered by reference to canon 6, n. 3, which legislates that the new law is to be judged by the old law in as far as the new agrees with the old. The old law forbade the priest to celebrate more than one mass a day. Though the term "*sacerdos*" was used, Honorius III[23] made it clear that the term included all priests, no matter to what dignity they were promoted: "*cuilibet sacerdoti quacumque dignitate praefulgeat.*"

Arregui teaches that bination is permissible "*probabiliter*" for the purpose of administering Holy Viaticum, even when—which would usually be the case—the ablutions have been taken in the first mass. There is no positive indication in the Code that this probable opinion must be given up. The probability is perhaps somewhat diminished by a slightly perceptible tendency of the new legislation toward a stricter attitude on the faculty of bination.[24]

In the faculties, which our Ordinaries formerly received, the article on bination contained a condition of a prohibitory nature, placed quite prominently in the article itself. The condition read as follows: *Celebrandi bis in die, si necessitas urgeat, ita tamen ut in prima Missa non sumpserit ablutionem.* Canon 806 contains no mention of this prohibitory clause but the point is covered by Canon 808: *Sacerdoti celebrare ne liceat, nisi ieiunio naturali a media nocte servato.*

To discuss the natural fast required for the licit celebration of mass lies beyond the scope of this study. But since, in the matter of bination, the question as to the permissibility of saying a second mass—after the natural fast has been broken by taking the ablutions through inadvertence—occasionally arises, it will not be amiss to submit the query here to a brief consideration. The authors[25] agree that the obligation of the faithful to attend mass would not in itself be a sufficient excuse for saying a second mass after the ablutions had been taken in the first. However, other elements may enter the case that would be sufficient excuses, according to the authors. Arregui puts the matter concisely: *Licet sacerdoti non ieiuno celebrare si ex inadvertentia ieiunium fregerit, v. c. dum ablutiones sumit in prima missa, cum alteram debeat agere, et missam sine offensione vel dicteriis populi omittere nequeat.*[26]

### Punishment for Binating Without Permission

For disregarding the law of the Church concerning the celebration of more than one mass on the same day the Code prescribes that the Ordinary suspend the offender for a certain length of time. Canon 2321 reads as follows: *Sacerdotes qui contra praescripta can. 802, par. 1, 808, praesumpserint Missam eodem die iterare vel eam celebrare non ieiuni, suspendantur a Missae celebratione ad tempus ab Ordinario secundum diversa rerum adiuncta praefiniendum.* The regulation of canon 806, par. 1, forbids priests to say more than one mass a day unless they have an Apostolic indult or permission from the Ordinary of the place. It is principally the disregard of this precept that comes into consideration here in connection with the faculty of binating. Binating, therefore, without authorization, or at least presumed consent as in cases of necessity, is one of the objects of the penal legislation given in canon 2321.

The punishment to be inflicted by the Ordinary is, as indicated by the terms of the law, *ferendae sententiae.* A priest who violates knowingly and wilfully the regulation of canon 806, par. 1, is not *ipso facto* suspended, but will incur the suspension only if and when it is inflicted by the Ordinary. The term *"praesumpserint"* requires that to establish the guilt of the offender two elements be present in the punishable act: full knowledge and deliberation[27] if the interpretation given this term in canon 2229, par. 2, for *poenae latae sententiae* holds good for *poenae ferendae sententiae.*[28] According to the principle: *"In poenis benignior est interpretatio facienda"*[29] the term *"praesumpserint"* in canon 2321 likewise deserves to be interpreted as presupposing full knowledge and deliberation.

The infliction of the punishment is stated in preceptive form *"suspendantur."* Hence, to inflict the punishment is a matter of obligation, ordinarily speaking, once the guilt has been established according to the sense of canon 2321.[30]

The punishment to be inflicted is *temporary* suspension from the celebration of mass. Substantially, therefore, the punishment is determined by the Code. As to the element of time, the punishment is *"indeterminata,"* because that element is left to the judgment of the Ordinary.[31] While it appears from a first reading of the canon in question that the punishment to be inflicted is of a vindictive nature, there is no solid reason against viewing the suspension as possibly medicinal, also. Hence, for repeated disregard of the precept of the Church contained in canon 806, par. 1 (and the one in canon 808, likewise), the Ordinary could inflict suspension from the celebration of mass as a medicinal punishment to break the contumacy of the offender. This opinion is advanced here with some hesitancy, since it implies that canon 2321 contains a twofold punishment, the one of a vindictive, the other of a medicinal nature, which implication would seem somewhat opposed at least to the spirit, if not the letter, of canon 2219, par. 1: *In poenis benignior est interpretatio facienda.* The opinion will find a basis in the consideration that suspension can by its nature be of a vindictive and a medicinal quality, and will meet no formidable opposition in the terms of the canon (i. e. 2321).

The length of time through which the suspension is to last must be decided "*secundum diversa rerum adiuncta.*" Sole[32] states that the time limit of the suspension is to be defined "*attentis circumstantiis aggravantibus aut minuentibus moralem imputabilitatem.*" As said above, the term "*praesumpserint*" presupposes "*plenam cognitionem ac deliberationem*"[33] and therefore precludes the consideration of an increased or diminished moral imputability. The words "*diversa rerum adiuncta*" apply, not to the personal guilt, for that seems weighed by the term "*praesumpserint,*" but to external circumstances of a personal or a non-personal nature, such as the frequency of the disregard, the scandal given, and so forth.

The term "*praefiniendum*" implies that the time limit of the suspension from the celebration of mass must be definite and mentioned in the oral or written infliction of the punishment. This would hold good, of course, only for the case in which suspension is inflicted as a vindictive punishment. From the use of the term "*praefinitum*" in connection with other specifications of suspension in canon 2298, no. 2,[34] it is evident that "praefiniendum" in canon 2321 excludes a suspension "*in perpetuum*" and a suspension "*ad beneplacitum Superioris.*"

## Notes

### IV

1. C. 3, 12, X, *de celebratione missarum, et sacramento Euchariatiae, et divinis officiis,* III, 41.
2. C. 12, X, *de celebratione, etc.,* III, 41.
3. We recall here what has been said in the general remarks on faculties, namely, that faculties serve also the subjective purpose of quieting those who are justly exempt from the strict observance of the law.
4. *De Syn. Dioec.* L. VI, cap. VIII, n. 2.
5. We are not considering here the possibility of the granting of this faculty through an apostolic indult.
6. See Noldin, *Summa Theol. Mor.,* III, p. 246, sq.
7. Gasparri, *De Sanctissima Eucharistia,* vol. I, p. 272, Paris, 1897.
8. Vol. VI, p. 568.
9. Gasparri, *op. cit.* I, p. 274.
10. *Op. cit.,* I, p. 277.
11. Cf. D'Annibale, *Sum. Theol. Mor.,* n. 405, footnote 55; Cappello, *De Sacr.* I, p. 595.
12. The homily is read in the breviary on the Feast of Christmas. "*Quia largiente Domino, Missarum solemnia ter hodie celebraturi sumus, loqui diu de evangelica lectione non possumus.*" Hom. 8 in Evang.
13. C. 3, X *de celebr.* III, 41.
14. *Quod expensis,* 27 Aug. 1748.
15. *Incruentum,* 10 Aug. 1915.
16. Compare *Instructio,* S. C. de Prop. Fide, May 24, 1870, n. 5, and *Declarasti Nobis* March 16, 1746, par. *Igitur omittentis.*
17. Cf. Sebastiani, *Summarium Theol. Moralis,* 1919, p. 250; Cappello, *De Sacr.* I, p. 594.
18. *Op. cit.,* p. 304.
19. January 12, 1847.
20. January 28, 1688.
21. No. 2827.
22. Cappello, *op. cit.,* I, p. 594.
23. C. 12, X *de celebr.* III, 41.
24. Arregui, *op. cit.,* p. 364; Cappello, *op. cit.,* p. 596.
25. Gasparri, *op. cit.,* vol. I, page 309; Putzer, *op. cit.,* p. 272; S. Alph. *Theol. Mor.,* VI, n. 287; Cappello, *op. cit.* I, p. 378.
26. *Op. cit.,* p. 346.
27. Can. 2229, par. 2.

28. Cf. Sole, *De Delictis et Poenis*, p. 242.
29. Can. 2219, par. 1.
30. Can. 2223, par. 3.
31. Canon 2217, par. 1, no. 1.
32. *Op. cit.*, p. 243.
33. Can. 2229, par. 2.
34. *Suspensio in perpetuum vel ad tempus praefinitum, vel ad beneplacitum Superioris.*

## V

## FACULTAS INCIPIENDI CELEBRATIONEM MISSAE UNA HORA ANTE AURORAM VEL UNA HORA POST MERIDIEM

The formulas of faculties formerly conceded the celebration of mass one hour *before daybreak* and one hour *after noon*. This concession is now a matter of common law.[1]

"*Aurora*," daybreak, precedes the rising of the sun by a considerable time (e. g. in the Eastern part of the United States by about 1½ hours in winter and 2 hours in summer). "Meridies," noon, is associated in our minds with a definite hour which hour may vary according to the different times (e. g. standard or sun). Daybreak, of course, is not associated with a definite hour, because of the ever-varying time of its occurrence.

Canon 33 permits us to follow any established or accepted time in the private celebration of mass.[2] For the public celebration of mass we must follow the common time of our locality for the obvious reason of order.[3]

For the sake of comparing present legislation concerning the celebration of mass with the concessions contained in Formula I, article XXIII of the former Faculties, quoted in full above at the beginning of the discussion of bination, we shall now consider several matters of importance in connection with the concessions made in that article.

### Mass "sine ministro"

The clause of the former faculty which permitted the celebration of mass without a server contained a concession the granting of which is beyond the power of the

Ordinary at the present time. Canon 813, par. 1 reads as follows: *Sacerdos Missam ne celebret sine ministro qui eidem inserviat et respondeat.* The obligation of having a mass server is considered a grave one by all authors. While the faculties formerly granted to our Ordinaries were still in force a *minor necessitas, quamvis aliqua*[4] was required to excuse the celebrant from the obligation of having a server. We have become so accustomed to look upon this obligation as less serious in this country that the opinion of authors on this point is felt as unacceptable in its full strength. Being accustomed for so long a time to a milder view of this obligation, in consequence of the former faculty, is a point that should not be overlooked. The unanimous opinion of authors on the gravity of the obligation was apparently based on conditions in countries where the Church was established well enough to get along conveniently without the faculties that were granted for missionary countries. The milder opinion, quite prevalent among priests in this country, will not be considered a refusal to accept the common opinion of authors on this matter.

It is not an altogether settled matter that the milder opinion is unjustifiable, especially in view of our legitimately acquired attitude towards the obligation. Even among the authors the obligation, grave as it was, was always qualified by "*per se.*" It will be well worth our while to recall that the opinion of some authors includes the permissibility of saying mass without a server so that the celebrant himself may fulfill the obligation of hearing mass *de praecepto.* In this instance the one obligation is weighed against the other. The obligation of hearing mass on the day of obligation is considered the more important of the two. And a *causa mediocriter gravis* excuses from the obligation of hearing mass on a day *de praecepto*. Surely a *causa mediocriter gravis* should suffice to exempt the celebrant from the obligation of having a server.

No doubt, it would be highly desirable if our Ordinaries were again granted the faculty of permitting the celebration of mass "*sine ministro.*" Such a concession would quiet the uneasy mind of many a celebrant.

## Regulations Concerning the Mass Server

Canon 813 requires a server who can serve and answer the prayers. A graver reason is required to say mass without a server than with one who does not know how to answer the prayers.

The second paragraph of canon 813 treats of the woman server: *Minister Missae inserviens ne sit mulier, nisi, deficiente viro, iusta de causa, eaque lege ut mulier ex longinquo respondeat nec ullo pacto ad altare accedat.* Formerly the Rubrics of the Missal positively forbade a woman to serve mass. In the course of time this prohibition became milder, and nuns were permitted by particular law to answer the prayers "*de longe*" but not to approach the altar for the purpose of performing the duties of the server, such as presenting the cruets, pouring the water at the Lavabo, and so forth.[5] The grant of particular law was extended by approved authors to the limits of the present general legislation. As is obvious from the term "*mulier*" the permission to answer the mass prayers is not limited to nuns or sisters. Serving at the altar is strictly forbidden, "*nec ullo pacto ad altare accedat.*" This does not forbid the woman who answers the prayers to ring the mass bell. The prohibition concerning serving at the altar is general and apparently comprehends sisters and nurses who would approach the altar to assist infirm or aged priests.

From the wording of canon 813, par. 2, it is apparent that there is no obligation to request a woman to answer the mass prayers, in the absence of a man server. On the contrary, there must be a good reason for permitting a woman to answer the prayers: *"nisi, deficiente viro, iusta de causa."* A good reason would be a long established custom, as is often the case in convents, or fear of offending or embarrassing a well-meaning person.

## The Place for Celebrating Mass.

As to the place where mass could exceptionally be celebrated, the former faculties granted the concession contained in the following words: *"sub dio et sub terra, in loco tamen decenti."* Canon 822, par. 4, of the New Code does not limit this faculty as to place except in so far as it forbids the celebration of mass *"in cubiculo."* It does limit the faculty, however, from a different angle, namely as to the frequency of application: *"in aliquo extraordinario casu et per modum actus."* The whole paragraph reads as follows: *Loci Ordinarius aut, si agatur de domo religionis exemptae, Superior maior, licentiam celebrandi extra ecclesiam et oratorium super petram sacram et decenti loco, nunquam autem in cubiculo, concedere potest iusta tantum ac rationabili de causa, in aliquo extraordinario casu et per modum actus.*

According to common law mass is to be celebrated: *"super altare consecratum et in ecclesia vel oratorio consecrato aut benedicto ad norman iuris."*[6] Canon 1191, par. 2 permits the celebration of mass in public oratories *"salvo contrario rubricarum praescripto."* Canon 1193, permits the celebration of mass in semi-public oratories *"nisi obstent rubricae aut Ordinarius aliqua exceperit."* The oratories of cardinals and bishops, residential or titular, enjoy all the rights and privileges of semi-public oratories.[7]

As to private oratories, a distinction is to be made. The Ordinary may grant, upon certain conditions, i. e.

upon visiting the oratories and finding them properly appointed, that even several masses may be celebrated in private cemetery chapels.[8] As to other private oratories, called domestic oratories, i. e. those erected in private homes for the use of the family or a private person, the Ordinary may grant permission to celebrate mass under very restricted terms: *"unius Missae, per modum actus, in casu aliquo extraordinario, iusta et rationabili de causa."*[9] And this permission may be granted only after the Ordinary or some other clergyman has visited the oratory and found it properly appointed.[10]

From the wording of canon 1194 it seems that in cemetery oratories mass may be celebrated quite frequently, though it is not evident that the ordinary can grant permission for daily celebration. If the latter were the case, the permission would most probably have been explicitly granted by common law.

The Ordinaries with the former faculties could grant the permission to say mass in private homes only on the condition: *"si aliter celebrari non possit."* A response of the S. Cong. de Prop. Fide, June 30, 1858 (which response is not given in the *Collectanea*), contains the following note concerning the point under consideration: *"Praeterea non ea est earundem facultatum extensio, qua Ampl. Tua quibusvis Sacerdotibus etiamsi aegrotis valeat permittere, ut in privatis aedibus super altari portatili Sacrum faciant."*[11] As Putzer[12] correctly teaches, it was not within the power of the Ordinary to permit the *habitual* celebration of mass in private homes.

Permission to celebrate mass daily in private oratories is a grant that must be obtained from the Holy See, i. e. from the Congregation of the Sacraments, or from the Apostolic Delegate.[13]

Even when an apostolic indult is granted certain limitations are to be observed unless the indult itself makes special concessions. Only one mass a day is allowed. On the more solemn feasts,[14] which are enumerated in the *Caeremoniale Episcoporum* II cap. XXXIV n. 2, mass is not permitted. The mass is always to be a low mass. The Ordinary himself or some delegated clergyman must first visit the private oratory and see whether it is properly appointed. The Ordinary could "*per modum actus*" permit mass on the above indicated feasts provided there were just and reasonable causes others than those that motived the indult. These various points are brought out carefully in Canon 1195. More than one mass could not be said in a private oratory on the same day unless the indult made special provision therefor.

The Ordinary can permit the celebration of mass outside the church or oratory on the condition that the mass be said "*super petram sacram et decenti loco.*" The altar stone is to be large enough so that the host and the greater part of the foot of the chalice can rest on it.[15] The place where mass is celebrated should be properly appointed.[16] The term "*decens*" permits of a broad interpretation, which the Ordinary himself could state in granting the permission or leave to the good judgment of others. A proper place means, of course, not only the locality or situation but also the various ornaments, furnishings, and equipment of the place. One place is expressly excepted by the Code, and that is the "*cubiculum,*" no matter how neatly and beautifully it be arranged. The term "*cubiculum*" no doubt means the bedroom.[17] The Code excludes the use of this room for the celebration of mass with the term "*nunquam.*" Hence, it would be useless to ask the Ordinary for the privilege of saying mass, e. g. in the bedroom of a sick person, in hospital wards, and the like, because such a grant is simply beyond the power of the Ordinary.

Those who have the privilege of a portable altar may celebrate mass anywhere, except at sea, and under the conditions given in canon 822, par. 3: *honesto tamen ac decenti loco et super petram sacram.* Gasparri[18] explains "*locus honestus*" as "*congruus Missarum celebrationi, mundus et convenienter ornatus.*"

The former faculty concerning the celebration of mass contained a very broad concession: "*Celebrandi . . . etiamsi altare sit fractum vel sine reliquiis sanctorum.*" As is evident from the interpretation of authors the "*altare fractum*" meant an "*altare enormiter fractum.*" The expression "*enormiter fractum*" goes back to regulations made by Innocent III.[19] It is used in the New Code, canon 1200, par. 2, n. 1. If an altar or an altar stone is broken to a great extent, "*enormiter,*" it loses its consecration and mass may not be celebrated thereon.

What is a "*fractura enormis*"? Authors agree that if the host and chalice cannot find room on one of the parts the "*fractura*" is "*enormis.*" If, however, there is place for the host and chalice on one of the parts, some hold the altar or altar stone is not broken "*enormiter.*" Gasparii[20] holds that as long as none of the crosses is broken off, the altar stone does not lose its consecration, provided there be enough space for the host and the chalice (or at least the greater part of the foot thereof). The New Code states that the "*fractura*" may be "*enormis*" either by reason of the size of the "*fractura*" or by reason of the place of unction, or, in other words, the place of the cross. The singular "*unctio*" seems to indicate that the stone loses its consecration if only one of the crosses is broken. Since this expression, however, also permits of a general interpretation, it is probably permissible to say mass on a stone even if one of the crosses is broken off.

The Ordinary has the power to permit a priest to reconsecrate, with the shorter rite and formula, an immovable altar which has lost its consecration by the separation of the altar table from the base.[21]

It is not permissible to say mass on an altar stone that does not contain the relics of Saints, according to liturgical prescript. The former faculty granted permission to say mass without the relics. It is beyond the power of the Ordinary now to permit mass "*super Altare fractum vel sine reliquiis.*" The broadest faculty granted him in this matter by the Code, namely in canon 822, par. 4, requires expressly: "*petra sacra.*" The stone is not sacred if it is broken—"*enormiter*"—or if it does not contain the prescribed relics.[22]

It is permissible to say mass on a consecrated altar of another rite "*deficiente altari proprii ritus.*" This privilege may not be used on the Greek "*antimensia.*"[23]

### Mass in the Presence of "Excommunicatus Vitandus."

The concession, in the former faculty, of celebrating mass "*praesentibus haereticis, schismaticis, infidelibus, et excommunicatis*" is as such no longer necessary. Today the "*excommunicatus vitandus*" is the only person in whose presence mass may not be said. Canon 2259, par. 2, reads as follows: ". . . *si vitandus* (*assistat*) *expellendus est, aut si expelli nequeat, ab officio cessandum, dummodo id fieri possit sine gravi incommodo.*"

The Code gives no special prescript as to the method of procedure in the case where such an excommunicated person enters the church during divine services. In view of the fact that the Church in its attitude toward the "*excommunicatus vitandus*" is inclined towards leniency, as is evident from a comparison of the Clementine legislation and the present Code in this matter,[24] it would seem permissible to give the clause of the Code "*dummodo id fieri possit sine gravi incommodo*" a rather lenient interpretation. Wernz[25] is inclined to take a mild view of the obligation of expelling the "*excommunicatus vitandus,*" or of discontinuing divine services when it is impossible to expel the intruder. He asserts that in our day such an obligation cannot be fulfilled without singular difficulty—perhaps he refers to the practical impossibility of applying physical force in the expulsion—and pleads for a milder discipline. The wording of the Code seems to indicate a realization of his wish.

The clause "*dummodo id fieri possit sine gravi incommodo*" applies principally, perhaps exclusively, to those attending divine services. The celebrant can in practically all cases discontinue services "*sine gravi incommodo*" as far as he himself is concerned, though, from a merely spiritual standpoint, there are conceivably some instances in which it would be a "*grave incommodum*" were he to deprive himself of the benefits or consolations of the sacrifice. There might be some cases, too, in which he would be obliged to continue services because of personal obligations, the non-fulfillment whereof would mean a "*grave incommodum*" to him.

If mass is to be discontinued, the celebrant should follow the prescript of the missal in an *a pari* instance: "*Si Sacerdote celebrante, violetur Ecclesia ante Canonem, dimittatur Missa: si post Canonem non dimittatur.*"[26] Gasparri[27] called attention to this prescript to dispute the probability of the opinion which permitted the celebrant to continue the mass only after consecration. He holds that if the canon of the mass is begun the celebrant should continue the mass, and leave the altar after communion "*cetera expleturus in sacrario.*"[28] Capello[29] teaches a method of procedure similar to that of Gasparri. Capello leaves it to the celebrant to continue or discontinue mass between the beginning of the canon and consecration.[30] All authors agree that if mass is continued the faithful are obliged to leave the church, with the exception of the mass server.

The Code itself gives no prescript as to the method of procedure in the case of inability to expel an "*excommunicatus vitandus.*"

## Notes

### V

1. The Rubrics of the Missal formerly permitted the celebration of mass at any hour *between* daybreak and noon.

2. Can. 33: *In supputandis horis diei standum est communi loci usui; sed in privata Missae celebratione, in privata horarum canonicarum recitatione, in sacra communione recipienda et in ieiunii vel abstinentiae lege servanda, licet alia sit usualis loci supputatio, potest quis sequi loci tempus aut locale sive verum sive medium, aut legale sive regionale sive aliud extraordinarium.* "Sidereal time will not answer for business purposes, because its noon occurs at all hours of the day in different seasons of the year. On the 22nd of September, for instance, it comes at midnight." Young, *Elements of Astronomy*, p. 35, 1919, New York. Sidereal time is, of its very nature, beyond the meaning of Canon 33, par. 1.

3. *Ex iusta causa, citra dispensationem vel privilegium, licebit plus quam una hora ante auroram vel post meridiem celebrare: nempe, si die feriali, ob peculiarem alicui mysterio vel Sancto devotionem, populus, qui postea agris excolendis vel industriae in opificiis vacare debet, consuevit vel velit sacro adesse; si sacerdos ex itinere arripiendo vel arrepto prohibeatur die festo ne debita hora celebret; in funeribus sollemnibus, in matrimoniis, occasione ordinationis, praedicationis, publicae supplicationis; si Missa sollemnis post meridiem protrahitur, licet ex consuetudine Missam privatam post eam celebrare, ne populi pars Missa careat; ad moriturum communicandum, licebit statim post mediam noctem celebrare.* Sebastiani, *op. cit.*, 451.

4. Sabetti, *Comp. Theol. Mor.* ed. 1902, p. 509.

5. S. C. R. Aug. 27, 1836.

6. Can. 822, par. 1.

7. Canon 1189.

8. Canon 1194.

9. *Ibid.*

10. *Ibid.*

11. Putzer, *op. cit.*, p. 281.

12. *Op. cit., loc. cit.*, p. 280.

13. The faculty of His Excellency on this point reads as follows: *Concedendi sacerdotibus infirmis durante infirma valetudine, aut aetate devexis indultum Oratorii privati, in quo Missam celebrent servatis canonicis regulis.* No. 35.

14. Gasparri, *op. cit.*, I, p. 166.

15. Can. 1198, par. 3.

16. Gasparri, *op. cit.*, I, p. 194.

17. Sebastiani, *op. cit.*, p. 249, footnote: *Cubiculum heic intelligitur locus, ubi cubilia seu lecti sunt.*

18. *Op. cit., loc. cit.*

19. C. 3, 6, X, III, 40.

20. *Op. cit.*, vol. I, p. 244.

21. Can. 1200. For this "*ritus brevior*" see the S. R. C. n. 3586.

22. What about the permissibility of celebrating mass on an altar stone that is not broken, but only cracked? If the crack runs across the center of the stone, there is no doubt but that the consecration of the stone is lost. The Cong. of Holy Rites has settled this point. (Sancti Hippolyti Aug. 31, 1861, n. 3162.) *"Aliqua etiam altaria portatilia, licet nec sepulcrum fuerit violatum nec enormis fractura adsit, tenui scissura laborant, quae per medium integrum lapidem decurrit. Quaeritur an per eiusmodi tenuem scissuram, ad instar fili, Altare execratum censendum sit?"* The Congregation gave an affirmative reply. It is doubtful whether a crack running across, say, one or more of the crosses, would cause the stone to lose its consecration. Abstracting from the consideration that such a crack is hardly *"enormis,"* one could point to a regulation in canon 1200, par. 3, which legislates on a quite similar question: *Levis fractio operculi non inducit execrationem et quilibet sacerdos potest rimulam cemento firmare.* Compare can. 1200, par. 2, n. 2.

23. Can. 823, par. 2. Mass may not be celebrated in "ecclesia violata." Cf. canons 1172, 1173. The reconciliation of an "ecclesia violata" is to take place according to the norm of canons 1176, 1177. The territorial Ordinary may delegate a priest to reconcile a consecrated Church. Cf. canons 1156, 1176, 1177.

24. C. 2 *de sent. excom.* etc., V, 10 in Clem.

25. *Op. cit.*, VI, p. 200, footnote 290.

26. *"De Defectibus in celebratione,* etc.*"* X, 2.

27. *Op. cit.*, II, p. 221.

28. *Loc. cit.*

29. *De Censuris*, p. 42, footnote 4.

30. Cf. S. Alphonsus, *op. cit.*, VII, 177.

## VI

## FACULTAS APPLICANDI MISSAM PRO POPULO, IUSTA DE CAUSA, ALIA DIE AB EA QUAE IURE STATITUR

In connection with the general question of the celebration of mass, it seems appropriate to treat of the permission which the Ordinaries may give their parish priests to transfer, that is, to anticipate or postpone the application of the *"Missa pro populo."*[1]

A prerequisite for the granting of the permission under consideration is a "just cause." The decision as to what constitutes a just cause rests, of course, with the Ordinary, as is evident from the wording of the law. The *"iusta causa" could be definitely stated in the* diocesan statutes or in a decree issued by the Ordinary. The official statement would then serve as a guidance in the use of the faculty. Formerly under the common law, the Ordinary could permit parish priests who were in great need to transfer the *missa pro populo* from the appointed day to some other day of the week, if that concession was of advantage to them. An apostolic indult was necessary for a dispensation in this matter for any other case outside that of poverty. Hence the present law, canon 466, par. 3, is a new and broad concession. A funeral, a wedding or an event of similar importance could be considered as a just cause, especially in those parishes in which the pastor is the only priest in charge.

It is not necessary to enumerate here the days on which the *missa pro populo* is to be said. They are to be found in the usual textbooks of moral theology or of canon law. The diocesan "Ordo" designates them in some practical manner. The Code does not say how soon the transferred mass is to be said. The *Cum semper oblatas* required that the transferred masses be said within a week. The same norm *could* be followed and the anticipated or postponed obligation fulfilled on a day near that designated by law.

## Notes

### VI

1. From a reply, dated Sept. 26, 1921, of Cardinal Gasparri, head of the Pontifical Commission for the Authentic Interpretation of the Canons of the Code, to His Excellency, the Apostolic Delegate of the United States, concerning the erection and status of parishes, it is plainly deducible that our parishes are to be considered ecclesiastical benefices.

2. Gasparri, *De SS. Eucharistia,* I, page 376; Wernz, *op. cit.* III, 2, p. 170; both these authors seem to assume that this faculty was of common law. The power for this special case of poverty of the parish priest is based on the *Cum semper oblatas* of Benedict XIV, Aug. 19, 1744. This constitution was sent to the Ordinaries of Italy.

## VII

## FACULTAS DEFERENDI PRIVATIM SACRAM COMMUNIONEM AD INFIRMOS

In the ordinary faculties that used to be granted to our bishops in Formula I, the faculty concerning the celebration of mass was followed *propter connexionem materiae* by the faculty concerning the bringing of Holy Communion to the sick, which read as follows: *Deferendi SSmum Sacramentum occulte ad infirmos sine lumine.* The concession, that was thereby granted, is now contained in canon 847: *Ad infirmos publice sacra communio deferatur, nisi iusta et rationabilis causa aliud suadeat.* A slight cause will suffice, says Cappello,[1] such as *"maius commodum infirmi aut familiae vel ipsius ministri."*

Canon 849 prescribes that in the private ministration of communion to the sick the regulations laid down by the Apostolic See are to be observed. These regulations are summed up in a decree of the Sacred Congregation of the Sacraments[2] which quotes Benedict XIV[3]: *Sacerdos stolam semper habeat propriis coopertam vestibus; in sacculo seu bursa Pyxidem recondat, quam per funiculos collo appensam in sinu reponat; et numquam solus procedat, sed uno saltem fideli, in defectu clerici, associetur.* There is no clause in the preceding decree or in the rubric of the Rituale Romanum[4] that would forbid placing the burse in a coat or vest pocket, provided the regulations given above are strictly observed. And it might be added that by placing the burse in an inside coat or vest pocket—*"supra pectus"* of course, and *"per funiculos collo appensam (scl. bursam)"*—the regulations stated by the Ritual *"ad pectus allegare," "obstringere"* are more easily observed, and with greater safety.[5]

A cleric or a layman should accompany the priest on such sick calls. If a cleric or a layman cannot be had, and there is question of administering Holy Viaticum in danger of death, the priest may go alone.[6] Whether a woman could or should follow (or precede) the priest on sick calls for administering the sacrament of Holy Communion, depends on the individual case in its local surroundings and the customary proprieties.

The speculative question as to why the phrase "*sine lumine*" appears in the former faculties, since the term "*occulte*" seems sufficient, may find its solution in the answer that the carrying of lighted candles was the principal indication of the presence of the Blessed Sacrament. The omission of this phrase in the regulations of Benedict XIV and of the S. Congregation of the Sacraments as given above made the use of it in the faculties superfluous as such, though its presence served as a reminder of its importance on occasion of the public ministration of Holy Communion to the sick.

The former faculties granted the permission "*retinendi—sine lumine—SSmum Sacramentum—pro eisdem infirmis, in loco tamen decenti, si ab haereticis aut infidelibus sit periculum sacrilegii.*" The Code has legislated on this point as follows: *Nemini licet sanctissimam Eucharistiam apud se retinere aut secum in itinere deferre.*[7] In canon 1269 the law is laid down as to the place where the Blessed Sacrament is to be kept. To make use of the concession in the former faculties, just mentioned, permission must be obtained from the Holy See.[8]

## Notes

### VII

1. *Op. cit.*, p. 320.
2. *Romana et aliarum*, 23 Dec. 1912.
3. *Inter omnigenas*, 2 Febr. 1744, par. 21, in Coll. S. C. de Prop. Fide, no. 345.
4. Tit. IV, c. 4, n. 10: *Quod si longius, aut difficilius iter obeundum sit, et fortasse equitandum, necesse erit vas, in quo Sacramentum defertur, bursa decenter ornata, et ad collum appensa, apte includere, et ita ad pectus alligare, atque obstringere, ut neque decidere, neque pixide excuti Sacramentum queat.*
5. Compare Wapelhorst, *Compendium Sacrae Liturgiae*, ed. 1904, p. 442, footnote 9.
6. Gasparri, *op. cit.* II, p. 349.
7. Can. 1265, par. 3.
8. *Salvo meliori iudicio.* Cf. Blat, *Comment. Text. Iuris Can.*, Lib. III, pars I, *De Sacramentis*, p. 768, ed. 1920; Cappello, *De Sacramentis*, I, p. 269, sq., ed. 1921.

## VIII

## FACULTAS BENEDICENDI SACRAM SUPELLECILEM ET PARAMENTA, QUAE AD NORMAM LEGUM LITURGICARUM BENEDICI DEBENT

This faculty is granted by common law to the parish priest for the churches and oratories within the territory of his parish and to rectors for their churches.[1] Other priests who receive the above stated faculty from the local Ordinary may use it, as the Code legislates expressly, within the limits of the delegation and of the jurisdiction of the delegating Ordinary.[2] The blessings in which an "*unctio sacra*" is prescribed, properly called "*consecrationes,*" can be validly given only by the bishop, unless permission therefor is granted by common law or apostolic indult.[3]

### Notes

VIII

1. Canon 1304, par. 3.
2. Canon 1304, par. 4.
3. Canon 1147, par. 1.

## IX

## FACULTAS AUDIENDI CONFESSIONES FIDELIUM UTRIUSQUE SEXUS

The faculty of hearing confessions is to be considered in practical importance and frequency of use next to the faculties concerning the Sacrament of the Holy Eucharist. In questions concerning the care of souls it is among the first that claim our attention. It is the object of the following pages to lay stress upon the principal points of practical value of Canon Law in its relation to the faculty of hearing confessions and to concomitant questions.

This faculty is usually contained in terms as "*audiendi confessiones,*" "*excipiendi*" or "*recipiendi confessiones,*" "*absolvendi a peccatis,*" or also in a general term such as "*administrandi omnia Sacramenta, Confirmatione et Ordine exceptis.*" The terminology for "*absolutio a peccatis,*" used by the Code in its canons on the question of penitential jurisdiction, is limited almost exclusively to the few specific terms given above. From a careful examination of these canons it is obvious that the terms are used synonymously.

The parish priest "*aliique qui loco parochi sunt*" do not need the faculty of hearing confessions in their own territory, since they have ordinary jurisdiction in this matter. Canon 873 states that point expressly, though it seems to be easily deducible from canon 197, par. 1, in connection with such canons that deal with the parish priest's office, namely "*cura animarum.*"

The ordinary jurisdiction of hearing confessions holds good for the territory of the pastor and those priests "*qui loco parochi sunt.*"[1] Barrett[2] claims that parish priests can, by reason of an almost universal custom, hear confessions in the whole diocese unless the bishop ordains otherwise. Arregui[3] does not commit himself on this point but is contented with referring to the teaching of Ferreres who holds the above mentioned opinion as probable.[4] He thinks that the former discipline in this matter has not been changed by the Code.

For the parish priests in this country this question is of no practical value. The grant of faculties gives our parish priests at least delegated jurisdiction for the rest of the diocese. The only case of practical importance that could depend on the theoretical solution of this question is one in which the renewal of faculties has been neglected. In such an instance the parish priest could appeal to the opinion given above. While this solution of the case just mentioned is offered in deference to the authority of Sabetti-Barrett, it is doubtful as to whether the extention of ordinary jurisdiction beyond parish lines is to be considered in last analysis as ascribable to the strength of custom or to the force of the diocesan faculties.[5]

That the ordinary jurisdiction of hearing confessions may be applied in absolving "*subditos ubique terrarum*" is established in canon 881, par. 2. Hence, faculties are not needed for such cases.

That the parish priest cannot delegate his ordinary jurisdiction of hearing confessions is now settled beyond dispute. The following question was placed before the Pontificial Commission for the authentic interpretation of the canons of the Code: *Utrum ad norman canonum* 199, *par.* 1, et 874 *par.* 1, *Parochi, Vicarii Parochorum, aliive sacerdotes ad universitatem causarum delegati, possint sacerdotibus sive saecularibus sive religiosis delegare iurisdictionem ad confessiones recipiendas, aut saltem iisdem iam approbatis iurisdictionem extendere ultra fines loci vel personarum, intra quos ad norman can.* 878, *par.* 1 *fuerit circumscripta; an ad id egeant speciali facultate seu mandato Ordinarii loci.* To this query the Commission replied: *Negative ad primam partem, affirmative ad secundam.*[6]

The Ordinary's power to confer delegated jurisdiction to hear confessions may be delegated by him to others, because that power is *ordinaria* and hence may be delegated according to canon 199, par. 1. The advisability of such delegation depends, of course, on the existing conditions in the place for which such a faculty is to be granted. It would be quite convenient, for more than one reason, if pastors were granted the faculty of conferring jurisdiction for hearing confessions to visiting priests who are in good standing or have full faculties in their own diocese. This is especially true in smaller places where the pastors are the *confessarii ordinarii* of the Sisters in charge of the school.

It is perhaps of theoretical value, only, to note that the Ordinary in granting the faculty of conferring delegated jurisdiction is thereby not granting the faculty of hearing confessions. Theoretically speaking, therefore, a deacon or a priest without the jurisdiction, delegated or ordinary, of hearing confessions could be chosen by the Ordinary to confer delegated jurisdiction for hearing confessions. The conferring of such jurisdiction is of course an act of ecclesiastic jurisdiction and requires as such a cleric agent.[7] Hence, a lay person could not grant delegated jurisdiction. But the delegation could be directed through the choice or medium of a lay person to any priest whose qualifications would meet the requirements of the delegation.

### Confessions of Religious Women

The general faculty of hearing confessions does not include the jurisdiction for hearing the confessions of nuns, sisters and their novices.[8] The special jurisdiction, mentioned in canon 876, is not required for hearing the confessions of women living in a community without the usual vows, for they do not properly come under the designation *"religiosae."*[9]

The law that restricts the general jurisdiction mentions the exceptions to the restrictions. It refers to the special privilege in this matter, granted to Cardinals. They enjoy ordinary jurisdiction for hearing the confessions *"religiosorum utriusque sexus"* in any part of the world.

### Canon 522

Another exception to the restriction of the general jurisdiction is that of canon 522, which makes a liberal provision for the confessions of religious women, in addition to the prescripts of other canons. This canon legislates as follows: "If notwithstanding these prescripts a religious woman, '*aliqua religiosa,*' for the peace of her conscience, goes to a confessor who has been approved by the Ordinary of the place for hearing women's confessions, the confession made in any church or oratory, even in a semi-public one, is valid and licit; every privilege to the contrary is revoked; the Superioress has no right to forbid such a confession or to make inquiries about same, even indirectly; religious women are not obliged to render the Superioress an account about such a confession." The prescripts of canon 520 and canon 521 refer to such confessors, ordinary and extraordinary, as have the special jurisdiction required by canon 876, par. 1.

The phrase *"ad suae conscientiae tranquillitatem"* has given rise to some dispute as to its bearing on the validity of the confession. For the present, at least, it is safe to follow the opinion of those who hold that the phrase is not *"ad validitatem."*

The clause *"adeat confessarium"* of canon 522 is interpretable from the answer of the Pontifical Commission, Nov. 24, 1920, as *"peragere confessionem apud confessarium."*[10] Hence, it is not necessary *to go to* a confessor. He could be called to the convent for the purpose of hearing a confession or confessions according to the norm of canon 522. It is within the power of the Ordinary, of course, to establish regulations that would prevent the abuse of the privilege, such as the law provides in a similar case in canon 520, par. 2.[11]

*"Confessarius ab Ordinario loci pro mulieribus approbatus"* is an expression that does not require a *specific* approbation for the confessions of women. A term such as *"pro utroque sexu approbatus"* would obviously suffice.[12] The Code requires that the approbation come from the *Ordinarius loci.* Cardinals do not need the approbation of the local Ordinary, since canon 239, par. 1, n. 1 grants them the broad faculty *"audiendi ubique terrarum confessiones, etiam religiosorum utriusque sexus."* But what is to be said about the *approbation* of the local Ordinary for those who have ordinary jurisdiction, such as the *"canonicus poenitentiarius," "parochus aliique qui loco parochi sunt?"* Fanfani[13] solves the difficulty in the following manner: *"Dependenter ab Ordinario loci—munera exercent; ergo in favorabilibus vere possunt dici confessarii ab Ordinario loci approbati pro omnibus fidelibus."* It seems more plausible to say that those in possession of ordinary jurisdiction can *a fortiori* hear the confessions in question. The sense of the expression seems to imply that a confessor approved by the local Ordinary at least for the confessions of women should be approached when the privilege of canon 522 is exercised.

*Approbation,* as it was understood in pre-Code legislation, no longer exists.[14] The present meaning of approbation in reference to the sacrament of Penance can perhaps best be gained from canon 882: *In periculo mortis omnes sacerdotes, licet ad confessiones non approbati, valide et licite absolvunt quoslibet poenitentes a quibusvis peccatis aut censuris,* etc. Approbation covers at least the concept of jurisdiction.[15] For the proper understanding of approbation in canon 522 it is only necessary to know that the term is now at least the equivalent of jurisdiction.

The limit of the privilege as to place is couched in very liberal terms: *in qualibet ecclesia vel oratorio etiam semipublico.* This expression includes therefore the churches and oratories, public or semi-public, not only "*extra propriam domum,*"[16] but also "*intra propriam domum.*"[17]

Among the doubts proposed to the Pontifical Commission for the authentic interpretation of the canons of the Code we find the following one referring to the requirement of place in canon 522. The doubt with its solution is here quoted in full: *De Religiosis, Dubium III: Utrum verba canonis* 522: *confessio in qualibet ecclesia vel oratorio etiam semipublice peracta valida et licita est: ita intelligenda sint, ut confessio extra ea loca peracta non tantum illicita, sed etiam invalida sit.—Resp. canon 522 ita est intelligendus, ut confessiones, quas ad suae conscientiae tranquillitatem religiosae peragunt apud confessarium ab Ordinario loci approbatum, licitae et validae sint, dummodo fiant in ecclesia vel oratorio etiam semipublico, aut in loco ad audiendas confessiones mulierum legitime destinato.*[18]

From this reply of the Pontifical Commission it is to be deduced that the terms of canon 522 referring to the place for confession were intended to mean that the confessions in question would be both licit and valid as long as the confessions were made in a place legitimately assigned to confessions of women. The lawgiver intended the possibility of a liberal interpretation, which would include not only the edifices or rooms, dedicated to divine worship according to law, and in which as a rule confessionals for confessions of both sexes, or of women only, were erected, but also those places in which the use of confessionals for women is authorized by law. The object of the lawgiver in mentioning the requirement of place was to stress the need of observing the regulations of canon law concerning the place for hearing the confessions of women, just as in mentioning the confessor in canon 522, the lawgiver calls attention to the requirement of jurisdiction for hearing the confessions of women. In the interpretation of *"locus ad audiendas confessiones mulierum legitime destinatus"* a moderate view is likewise to be taken, that is, the mind of the legislator, rather than the letter of the law, is to be the norm of interpretation.

The expression of the above reply: *"in loco ad audiendas confessiones mulierum legitime destinato"* seems interpretable as including any place which under given conditions[19] is permissible for the purpose of hearing the confessions of women. The conditions which permit the hearing of the confessions of women outside the confessional and, hence, outside the *"locus patens et conspicuus"*[20] are given in canon 910, par. 1: *Feminarum confessiones extra sedem confessionalem ne audiantur, nisi ex causa infirmitatis aliave verae necessitatis, et adhibitis cautelis quas Ordinarius loci opportunas iudicaverit.*[21] The term *infirmitas* means, in general, physical inability to comply with the regulation of using the confessional. Deafness and decrepit old age would likewise come under this heading.[22] Other causes of real necessity, *"verae necessitatis,"* would also excuse from the observance of the regulation, provided the *"cautelae,"* if such have been established by the Ordinary, are used.

The *"cautelae"* to be used in the exceptional cases, mentioned in canon 910, par. 1, could consist of such directions that would safeguard the privacy of confession and at the same time disarm suspicious minds.[23]

The practical question whether the confessions of nuns or sisters could be heard in the parlor depends for its solution on the fulfillment of the conditions or qualifications required by the Code for the place where the confessions are to be heard. If, therefore, the parlor is a *"locus patens et conspicuus"* the confessions of nuns and sisters could be heard there. It is presupposed, of course, that the confessions are heard in a confessional, unless, as said above, infirmity or some other good reason exempt from the regulation of using a confessional.

It is superfluous to consider at length the other places that come within the law for the confessions of women. The proper place for sacramental confession is, as canon 908 legislates, the church or the oratory, public or semi-public. The term *"proprius"* allows some latitude for private oratories or other places that meet the requirements of the law, but also implies the wish of the Church that the sacrament of Penance be administered in a church of oratory, public or semi-public. The confessional for women, or which serves for hearing the confessions of women also, should always be placed *"in loco patenti et conspicuo," "et generatim in ecclesia vel oratorio publico aut semipublico mulieribus destinato."*[24] Blat [25] refers the last qualification *"mulieribus destinato"* to a semi-public oratory, which is not exclusively assigned to men, though even in a semi-public oratory assigned exclusively to men the confessions of women could be heard by way of the exception provided for in the term *"generatim."* Regulations concerning the grate of the confessional are prescribed in canon 909, par. 2. Whether both the places where the priest sits for hearing confessions and the place where the penitent kneels are to be *"in loco patenti et conspicuo"* is not evident from the wording of the law, but the intention of the lawgiver would seem carried out if only the former be in an open and visible place.

The Code revokes any and all privileges granted to religious institutes of women, that would in any way hinder the exercise of the privilege now granted by canon 522. To strengthen the privilege the same canon legislates against any interference whatsoever on the part of the Superioress.[26]

### Canon 523

The last exception to the law requiring special jurisdiction for hearing the confessions of nuns and sisters (can. 876, par. 1) is the concession made in canon 523. This privilege grants to all sisters and nuns, who are seriously sick, though not dangerously so, the right to call in any priest approved for hearing the confessions of women, even though he is not appointed for the confessions of religious, and to confess to him as often as they wish, during the time of their serious illness. The Superioress is not allowed to interfere in this right either directly or indirectly.

This privilege is taken almost word for word from the decree of the S. Cong. for Religious, Feb. 3, 1913.[27] Canon 523 requires that the priest be approved for hearing the confessions of women, but states expressly that he need not be assigned for the confessions of religious. The decree, in the paragraph referring to this privilege, does not contain the prescript against the interference on the part of the Superioress.

The concession embodied in canon 523 differs in several important points from the privilege granted in canon 522. Canon 523 refers to nuns and sisters who are seriously sick. Canon 522 refers principally to those who are in good health or are in condition to go to confession *"in loco ad audiendas confessiones mulierum legitime destinato,"* but includes also, according to the interpretation given above, those religious women whose confessions may be heard outside the confessional *"ex causa infirmitatis aliave verae necessitatis."* Hence, canon 522 includes the "*religiosae leviter aegrotantes.*" Canon 523 does not require the condition of canon 522 "*ad suae conscientiae tranquillitatem.*" The restriction to the approval of the confessor "*ab Ordinario loci*" in canon 522 is omitted in canon 523. It is not improbable that this omission was intended to give the privilege a wider scope than that of canon 522. Such an interpretation might find some basis in the terms "*quemlibet sacerdotem—approbatum.*"

Canon 523 adds, moreover, the broad permission that during the time of the serious illness, the nuns or sisters in question may go to confession to the priest, they have called, as often as they desire. Instead of the terminology "*confessio valida et licita est,*" canon 523 uses the expression "*possunt confiteri.*" The various differences between the prohibition of interference in canon 522 and that of canon 523 must be considered especially in the case of penal procedure.[28]

Whatever is considered serious illness "in the common estimation of the people"[29] comes under the heading of "*gravis infirmitas.*" Papi[30] is inclined to include the period of convalescence from a serious illness.[31]

## Diocesan Reservations

Besides the limitation of jurisdiction in canon 876, par. 1, there are certain other restrictions which can be made by the *Superior* who confers the delegated jurisdiction or is empowered by law to except some cases from the ordinary jurisdiction, or which are established by the *Code* itself.

Delegated jurisdiction or, as is the case for the religious in certain instances, permission to hear confessions may be granted with restrictions.[32] Restrictions as to time are e. g. "*ad revocationem,*" "*ad annum,*" as to persons e. g. "*pro viris tantum,*" as to place, e. g. "*in tali paroecia tantum.*"[33]

The exercise of ordinary jurisdiction and *a fortiori* of delegated jurisdiction may be limited by reservations of sins and censures. The number of reserved sins should not exceed four.[34] The *canonicus poenitentiarius* has ordinary jurisdiction to absolve from such reserved sins, which jurisdiction cannot be restricted by the Ordinary, since it is granted *a iure.*[35] The power to absolve from sins reserved in the diocese should be given *"habitualiter"* to the rural deans with the faculty of subdelegation.[36] Parish priests and others who in law come under the name of parish priests[37] have ordinary jurisdiction to absolve from the sins which the Ordinary has reserved to himself in any manner, during the whole period in which the paschal precept may be fulfilled. Missionaries likewise enjoy ordinary jurisdiction for such reserved cases during the time of the mission.[38] All cases which the Ordinary reserves to himself lose their force[39] under the following circumstances: (1) In the case of sick people who cannot leave their homes, and in the case of those who are making a confession preparatory to marriage; (2) When the Superior refuses to grant the required faculty, or when it is impossible to obtain same without grave inconvenience for the penitent or without danger of violating the seal of confession; (3) Outside the territory of the Superior who has made the reservation, even though the penitent left the territory just for the purpose of obtaining absolution from the reserved sin.

The consideration of the legislation governing the establishment, nature and promulgation of reserved cases does not come within the scope of this study. Once such reservations are made by the Ordinary, both the ordinary and the delegated jurisdiction of confessors is limited accordingly. Usually the reserved sins are mentioned in the document or grant of diocesan faculties, and whatever concessions are made concerning the absolution from such sins, the terms or wording thereof and the *mens legislatoris* are of decisive value. The guiding principle in the interpretation of reservations and concomitant concessions is, of course: *Odiosa restringenda, favores ampliandi.*

## Absolutio Complicis

A relative limitation of penitential jurisdiction,[40] established by common law is contained in canon 884: *Absolutio complicis in peccato turpi invalida est, praeterquam in mortis periculo: et etiam in periculo mortis, extra casum necessitatis, est ex parte confessarii illicita ad normam constitutionum apostolicarum et nominatim constitutionis Benedicti XIV Sacramentum Poenitentiae.* This limitation was originally established in *Sacramentum Poenitentiae,* par. 4 in Document V attached to Code: *Omnibus et singulis sacerdotibus—auctoritate Apostolica, et Nostrae potestatis plenitudine interdicimus et prohibemus, ne aliquis eòrum extra casum necessitatis, nimirum ipsius mortis articulo, et deficiente tunc quocumqe alio sacerdote qui confessarii munus obire possit, confessionem sacramentalem personae complicis in peccato turpi atque inhonesto, contra sextum Decalogi praeceptum commisso, excipere audeat, sublata propterea illi ipso iure quacumque auctoritate et iurisdictione ad qualemcumque personam ab huiusmodi culpa absolvendam; adeo quidem, ut absolutio, si quam impertierit, nulla atque irrita omnino sit, tanquam impertita a sacerdote, qui iurisdictione ac facultate ad valide absolvendum necessaria privatus existit, quam ei per praesentes has Nostras adimere intendimus.* A confessor guilty of *complicitas in peccato turpi* is deprived of the jurisdiction of absolving his accomplice not only from the sin of complicity *in peccato turpi,* but of course also from other grievous sins which would have to be submitted to penitential jurisdiction at the same time. This privation of jurisdiction lasts as long as the sin of complicity remains a matter of direct absolution.

The first part of the canon pertains to the invalidity of the absolution; the second part, to the illicitness thereof under given conditions. If the last phrase ("*ad norman constitutionum apostolicarum et nomination constitutionis Benedicti XIV Sacramentum Poenitentiae*"), in the canon refers to both the first and the second part, then the usual text book interpretations still obtain. If, however, the phrase refers to the second part only, then the invalidity of the absolution will have to be interpreted primarily according to the mind of the legislator, as expressed in the present terms of the Code and not according to the terms of former apostolic constitutions.

From the construction of the canon one would judge that the phrase is intended to be a modification of the second part only. The constitution *Apostolici muneris*,[41] treats of the matter mentioned in the second half, but the constitution to which the canon refers "*nominatim*" treats of the restriction of jurisdiction only. Hence, it would appear that the phrase modifies both parts of the canon. *Salvo meliori iudicio*, the doubt as to the precise purpose of the modifying terms is sufficiently well founded to affect some of the views on the extent of the validity of the absolution in question.[42]

What is to be said of the case in which the confessor is not aware of the fact that he has no jurisdiction to absolve his accomplice, or that the penitent is his accomplice? Some authors[43] hold that the absolution is valid in both instances. The reasons they give for their view are the following: The legislation of *Sacramentum Poenitentiae* presupposes that the confessor is aware of the fact that he has no jurisdiction for the case in question and that the penitent before him is his accomplice, because the lawgiver uses the terms "*ne excipere audeat*," which exclude ignorance. Does this argument still hold good? If the modifying phrase "*ad normam, etc.*," governs the first part of the canon 884, the argument deserves some consideration, although even in the pre-Code legislation, namely in the fundamentally important *Sacramentum Poenitentiae,* the full text of the law in nowise seems to favor any exception for cases of ignorance. However, if the present wording of the first part of canon 884 is not dependent for its legislative interpretation on former constitutions, and is to be understood according to the value of the actual terms, then surely no defense for the validity of absolution in cases of ignorance is to be found in the present legislation. It is also to be noted that in a parallel case, namely, when the confessor does not know the law concerning the *absolutio complicis,* the absolution is nevertheless invalid.[44]

Another argument advanced by the side affirming the validity of the absolution is that the restriction of jurisdiction is a kind of punishment, and, hence, this privation or restriction is not incurred *"ab ignorantibus."* Neither the *Sacramentum Poenitentiae* nor the other constitutions contain any indication that the privation of jurisdiction is to be considered a penal sanction. The wording of the pertinent passages in the constitutions positively states that the purpose of the legislation is cautionary.[45] Privation of jurisdiction is not always or necessarily penal.[46] In what sense could the privation of jurisdiction be considered a punishment for those who never come in contact again with their accomplice? The limitation of jurisdiction *quoad complicem* is, *per se,* so insignificant, compared to the large number of penitents, actual or possible, that it seems inconsistent with the methods of legislation to consider so small an exception a commensurate punishment for so serious a crime.

The other opinion which holds that the absolution is invalid in the case of *"ignorantia sive quoad privationem iurisdictionis sive quoad personam complicis"* bases its arguments 1) on the wording of the law, as has been considered above in reply to the reasons of the affirmative side, and 2) on the fact that, at least in the instance where the confessor fails to recognize the penitent as his accomplice, the false subjective attitude does not change the objective effects of the law.[47] If it is admitted that the modifying phrase "*ad norman, etc.,*" refers only to the latter half of canon 884, as seems quite admissible from the grammatical construction thereof, then the opinion which considers the absolution invalid certainly seems favored by the Code.[48]

For an explanation of the terms "*complex in peccato turpi et inhonesto,*" the usual text book treatise on this matter is sufficiently thorough. By complicity in the present canon is understood any action or speech that is a "*peccatum certum, externum, grave contra sextum decalogi praeceptum*" committed *mutually* by two or more persons. It matters not whether the sin of complicity has been committed before or after ordination to the priesthood. The accomplice may be of either sex, and of any age after the use of reason has been attained. The use of reason is required as an element of the *complicitas formalis* and, of course, as a natural prerequisite of the moral responsibility.

The Code does not restrict the jurisdiction in danger of death. The *Sacramentum Poenitentiae* and the *Apostolici muneris* use the expression "*in ipsius mortis articulo,*" the *Apostolicae Sedis* uses "*in mortis articulo,*" and canon 2367, par. 1, "*in articulo mortis.*" In this last mentioned passage, canon 2367, par. 1, the term "*articulus mortis*" seems explained in the terms "*morientis*" and "*moribundus*" of the same canon. Cappello thinks that canon 884 prefers the term "*periculum mortis*" to "*articulus mortis.*"[49] There is nothing in canon 2367, par. 1, that could disprove this. It is worthy of notice that the Code, in canon 884, has not used the terms of the Apostolic constitutions "*in articulo mortis.*"

What is meant by *periculum mortis?* Chelodi[50] answers the question in the following words: *Quando mors est vere probabilis, sive ab intrinseco ut puta morbo, vulnere inflicto, partu difficili, extrema senecta; sive ab extrinseco, velut ex bello, navigatione periculosa et id genus ceteris.* Sole[51] quotes D'Annibale as teaching that the expression means: *illud rerum discrimen in quo et superesse et occumbere utrumque est vere graviterque probabile.* D'Annibale[52] had added to the foregoing the danger of falling into "*amentia perpetua.*" Cappello[53] also adopts the explanation of D'Annibale, which is substantially the teaching of St. Alphonse.[54] Most probably the Code implies a distinction between *periculum mortis* and *articulus mortis,* as seems deducible from a comparison of canon 884 and canon 2367, par. 1.[55]

However, even in danger of death, the absolution of an accomplice, though valid, is illicit under certain circumstances. The Code refers to the Apostolic constitutions and especially to the *Sacramentum Poenitentiae* for the norm according to which the illicitness is to be judged. Briefly stated, the circumstances mentioned are such that, if another priest, though he have no jurisdiction for hearing confessions, can be called without causing grave scandal or evil talk (*infamia*), the absolution granted by the *sacerdos complex* is *valid but illicit,* and the censure of canon 2367, par. 1, is incurred; likewise if the confessor *complex* makes the above mentioned dangers only appear as such[56], or if he has culpably neglected to avoid or remove them, then the absolution is valid but illicit, and the censure is incurred. Canon 884 does not mention the case in which the dying accomplice refuses to confess to some other priest, as given in the last clause of canon 2367, par. 1, since it provides for that in the phrases: *extra casum necessitatis, ex parte confessarii illicita.*

Some authors[57] permit (by *epikeia*) the *confessarius complex* to absolve the penitent in very grave necessity. The confessor is advised to ask the S. Poenitentiaria for the faculty of absolving the accomplice as soon as he becomes aware of the extreme necessity. The petition is sent with a fictitious name for the confessor for whom the faculty is asked. The confessor can write for himself in the third person. The formula for this petition is given by some authors as follows: *Titius sacerdos petit facultatem, quam alias nunquam petivit, absolvendi complicem. Causa est.*[58] . . . The Ordinary could not grant this faculty, unless he were delegated to do so.

### Falsa Accusatio de Sollicitatione

The restriction of jurisdiction, legislated in canon 884, relates to the individual confessor who is guilty of the *complicitas in peccato turpi.* Hence, it is rightly called a relative restriction. Canon 894 contains a restriction that is absolute as to persons and relative as to sins. It reads as follows: *Unicum peccatum ratione sui reservatum Sanctae Sedi est falsa delatio qua sacerdos innocens accusatur de crimine sollicitationis apud iudices ecclesiasticos.*

In the pre-Code legislation there was another sin reserved to the Holy See, namely, "*acceptatio munerum a regularibus utriusque sexus mortaliter mala.*"[59] This reserved case had practically gone into desuetude.[60] The Code has definitely abrogated the reservation by making the sin mentioned in canon 894 the only one *unicum peccatum,* reserved *ratione sui* to the Holy See.

The fundamental interpretation of canon 894 is to be found in the constitution *Sacramentum Poenitentiae.*[61] *Etsi pastoralis*[62] states that the law against solicitation obliges Latins and Greeks. *Apostolici muneris*[63] confirms in a general way only, the law of *Sacramentum Poenitentiae* against solicitation and false accusation connected therewith. Among other Roman documents the instruction of the Holy Office of Feb. 20, 1866 is the most extensive explanation of the law in question. The Code itself legislates on the subject of solicitation in several other canons, namely 904, 2362, 2368.

The sin of false accusation is reserved *ratione sui.* The expression *ratione sui* is understood to mean *ratione peccati,* in contradistinction to *ratione censurae.* Thus the authors. Whether that is the meaning intended by the Code remains to be seen.

The sin is reserved to the Holy See,[64] which in this instance is the Sacred Penitentiary, since the matter pertains to the internal forum.[65]

The person falsely accused is the priest, *sacerdos.* The laws does not use here the term *confessarius,* which presupposes jurisdiction for hearing confessions. Canon 2363 inflicts a censure for the false accusation of the confessor.

The legal concept of solicitation is best gained from the explicit and detailed terms of the *Sacramentum Poenitentiae* itself: *Mandamus . . ut . procedant contra omnes, et singulos sacerdotes . . . , qui aliquem poenitentem, quaecumque illa persona sit, vel in actu sacramentalis confessionis vel ante, vel immediate post confessionem, vel occasione, aut praetextu confessionis, vel etiam extra occasionem confessionis in confessionali, sive in alio loco ad confessiones audiendas destinato, aut electo, cum simulatione audiendi ibidem confessionem, ad inhonesta, et turpia sollicitare, vel provocare, sive verbis, sive signis sive nutibus, sive tactu, sive per scripturam, aut tunc aut post legendam, tentaverint, aut cum eis illicitos, et inhonestos sermones, vel tractatus temerario ausu habuerint.* In the quotation are found the details or time, place, manner and purpose.[66]

It is to be noted that canon 894 uses rather broad terms: *falsa delatio, qua—accusatur,* which leaves the cause, or agent, of the accusation undetermined. No reference is made to the *Sacramentum Poenitentiae*, or other documents, from which the interpretation of these terms is to be taken. In the *Sacramentum Poenitentiae* there is no room left for doubt as to what persons are to be considered the causes, or agents. The constitution states: *quaecumque persona, quae exsecrabili huiusmodi flagitio se inquinaverit, vel per se ipsam innocentes confessarios impie calumniando, vel sceleste procurando, ut id ab aliis fiat.*[67] Blat[68] teaches that direct and indirect causes, or agents, are meant by canon 894. In consideration of the benign principle: *odiosa sunt restringenda* and of the fact that the canon does not demand an interpretation according to the former documents legislating on this subject, it does not seem improbable that the legislator wanted the law restricted to those who directly or immediately make the false accusation.

It is to be noted that special stress is placed on the "*falsa delatio*" by the qualifying term "*innocens*" used in describing the person accused. The term "*innocens*" is to be interpreted as restricted to that single instance or those instances in which the crime of solicitation is asserted to have taken place. Even if from the investigation of the false accusation the fact developed that the accused priest had been guilty of the crime on some occasion other than the instance or instances mentioned in the false accusation, the sin would be reserved because of the "*falsa delatio*" of a definite instance in which the priest was not guilty.[69]

An essential clause of canon 894 requires that the accusation be made to *ecclesiastical judges.* Apparently this clause forms the principal distinction—most probably the only one of consequence—between canon 894 and canon 2363.[70] The latter canon speaks of a denunciation that is made to the Superiors, who are mentioned without any further qualifications. Sole[71] interprets the term Superiors to mean the local Ordinary or the S.

Congregation of the Holy Office according to canon 904. Capello interprets the term Superior (incidentally, he uses the singular) in the following manner: *intelligi debet non quilibet Praelatus, licet fortasse iurisdictione gaudeat in confessarium denuntiatum, sed iudex ecclesiasticus, is nempe, cuius est inquirere et procedere . . contra sollicitantes.*[72] The initial denunciation may be made to others besides the Ordinary, namely the chancellor of the Curia, the rural deans and the parish priests who are to transmit the denunciation to the Ordinary.[73]. There is no solid objection to considering these ecclesiastic persons the Superiors of the denunciator. Be that as it may, even when the denunciation is sent or made immediately to the local Ordinary, the judicial accusation cannot be considered as having taken place, though by reason of the ultimate purpose the denunciation could be called *iudicialis.* Noval[74] implies quite clearly a distinction between the initial denunciation, that is made to the local Ordinary, and the denunciation or accusation, that is made in the name of the accuser by the "*promotor iustitiae*" to the ecclesiastical judge.

*Salvo meliori iudicio,* the initial denunciation suffices to incur the censure of canon 2363, while only the accusation made to the ecclesiastical judge can cause the reservation legislated in canon 984. The reasons for this opinion are the following: In the first place the legal terminology selected by the lawgiver strongly favors that view. Canon 894 uses the term "accusation" and consistently therewith the term "ecclesiastical judges." Canon 2363 uses the term "*denuntiaverit*" and consistently therewith the term "*Superiores.*" Canons 1934, 1935, 1936, 1937 and 1955 support the conclusion based on the use of terms.[75]

Secondly, if the crime of canon 894 were identical with that of canon 2363, most probably some reference to that identity would have been made in the latter canon, as has been done in canon 2368, par. 1, or for the sake of precision the same terms would have been used.

Thirdly, at the end of canon 2363 is the phrase "*firmo praescripto can.* 894," which finds a plausible explanation only on the assumption that the crime of canon 894 and that of canon 2363 are two distinct transgressions. The phrase refers to the whole canon, according to the rule of interpretation: *quod clausula in fine referenda sit ad omnia praecedentia, nisi aliqua vel evidens vel saltem probabilis ratio contrarium suadeat.* Now the canon concluding with that phrase speaks of the censure and its cessation through absolution. If the crime of canon 894 is the sin censured in canon 2363, then according to canon 2246, par. 3: *si quis a censura excusatur vel ab eadem fuit absolutus, reservatio peccati penitus cessat,* the reservation of canon 894 should also cease. The cessation of that reservation, however, is explicitly excepted. Hence, the sin of false accusation made to ecclesiastical judges is not the same as the sin of false denunciation made to the Superiors.[76]

Consistently with the view that the false accusation of canon 894 is a distinct sin from the false denunciation of canon 2363, *salvo meliori iudicio*—the latter sin alone is punished with excommunication reserved in a special manner to the Holy See[77] and the former alone is reserved of its own account, *ratione sui,* to the same authority. It seems highly improbable that a double punishment would be inflicted for the same crime without some reference to the plurality of penal sanctions.

The question as to whether ignorance of the reservation of the sin reserved in canon 894, and, incidentally, of the other reservations, treated in the chapter *De reservatione peccatorum,* canons 893 to 900, inclusively, excuses from the reservation, seems so far an unsettled matter.[78] The weight of the solution rests apparently on the answer to the preliminary question as to whether the reservation of sins without censure is of a penal nature, at least primarily. The Code gives no direct reply to the question as to the penal nature of reservation of sin, nor does it state any explicit doctrine on the nature or effects of ignorance of reserved sin. The opinion of authors that favor the exemption from reservation in cases of ignorance, not gravely culpable, is to be followed in practice.[79]

In connection with the papal reservation of canon 894 the doubt is raised as to whether it also follows the regulations of canon 900. Blat[80] confines the legislation of the final canon on the reservation of sins to the reserved cases of the local Ordinaries only. Gearin,[81] understands *"quaevis reservatio"* to include the papal reservation also.[82]

## Notes

### IX

1. Can. 873, par. 1.
2. Sabetti-Barrett, *Compendium Theol. Mor.*, 27th ed., p. 739.
3. *Summarium Theol. Mor.*, 3rd ed., p. 390, footnote 1.
4. *Theol. Mor.*, II, p. 652.
5. Noldin approaches the difficulty in this manner (*Summa Theol. Mor.*, III, p. 404): *Ad cavendas difficultates usus habet, ut parochi........pro tota dioecesi approbationem et delegatam iurisdictionem accipiant.* Morino *Theol. Mor.* II, 7th ed., p. 352, admits that the custom exists in some dioceses. Cf. Augustine, *op. cit.* IV, p. 262; Eccles. Review, June, 1921, pp. 565, sqq.
6. Oct. 16, 1919.
7. Can. 118.
8. Can. 876, par. 1: *Revocata qualibet contraria lege seu privilegio, sacerdotes tum saeculares tum religiosi, cuiusvis gradus aut officii, ad confessiones quarumcunque religiosarum ac novitiarum valide et licite recipiendas peculiari iurisdictione indigent, salvo praescripto can.* 239, *par.* 1, *n.* 1, 522, 523.
9. Can. 673, par. 1.
10. Compare the same term *"adire confessarium"* in canon 2254, par. 2, and a similar expression in canon 1361, par. 1, and the extent of the latter in par. 2.
11. The expression *"adeat confessarium"* is most probably not to be considered as a requisite *ad validitatem*, since the reply of the Pontifical Commission Nov. 24, 1921, used so broad an expression: *"peragere confessionem apud confessarium."* Cf. opposite opinion in Comment. pro Religiosis, pp. 13, sqq. Jan. 1921.
12. Augustine, *op. cit.* III, page 163.
13. *Op. cit.*, page 59.

14. Slater, in The Eccl. Review, June, 1921, p. 563.

15. Blat, *op. cit.* III, pars. I, page 234.

16. Cf. Decree of S. Cong. de Religiosis, Feb. 3, 1913.

17. Blat, *op. cit.* II, p. 503; Augustine, *op. cit.* IV, p. 353; Papi, *The Government of Rel. Communities*, p. 139; Fanfani, *op. cit.*, p. 63, holds that canon 522 comprehends the churches and oratories of nuns and sisters, but adds: "*dummodo id (adire confessarium) fiat ad modum saecularium mulierum, in confessionali publico seu communi, et tempore quo ipsae saeculares mulieres possent, si velint, ad talem confessarium accedere. Ubi enim lex non distinguit, nec nos distinguere debemus.*" The principle just quoted would apparently invalidate Fanfani's restrictions. He continues: "*Nihilominus quod supradictae conditiones verificentur necessarium omnino videtur: secus, si cuilibet religiosae, semper ac habet possibilitatem, liceret quemcunque confessarium pro mulieribus approbatum, in propria ecclesia seu oratorio etiam semipublico, quocunque tempore et in ipso confessionali pro sororibus deputato adire, actum esset de confessariis ordinariis et extraordinariis pro ipsis.*" This unpleasant consequence would be obviated to a great extent by the cautious and prudent elimination of possible abuses through appropriate regulations given by the Ordinary, "*salva conscientiae libertate.*" Can. 520, par. 2.

18. Nov. 24, 1920.

19. Can. 910, par. 1.

20. Can. 909, par. 1.

21. Incidentally it is to be noted that there seems to be some reason why canon 909, par. 1 uses the term "*mulieres*" and canon 910, par. 1, the term "*feminae.*" *Salvo meliori iudicio*, these passages seem to imply that the confessions of all "*feminae,*" even the youngest, must be heard in a confessional, but that only the confessionals for the confessions of "*feminae post pubertatem*" are to be placed and erected according to the regulations of canon 909, par. 1. The Code itself makes no explicit distinction between "*feminae*" and "*mulieres,*" but the distinction appears deducible from a comparison of canons 88, par. 2, 1067, par. 1 and 2342 n. 2. Cf. Schaaf, *The Cloister*, Cincinnati 1921, p. 87.

22. S. Cong. de Prop. Fide, Sept. 21, 1840, ad 8.

23. S. Cong. de Prop. Fide, April 13, 1807, ad XIII: "*cubiculi ianua sit patefacta, ut conspici tam confessarius, quam paenitens possint.*"

24. Can. 909, par. 1.

25. *Op. cit.* III, pars. I, p. 284.

26. Cf. canon 2414.

27. *Moniales omnes aut Religiosae, cum graviter aegrotant, licet mortis periculum absit, quemlibet sacerdotem ad confessiones excipiendas adprobatum arcessere possunt, eique perdurante gravi infirmitate, quoties voluerint, confiteri.*

28. Canon 2414.

29. Papi, *op. cit.*, page 141.

30. *Op cit. loc. cit.*

31. The law technically states "*perdurante gravi infirmitate*" and not "*perdurante infirmitatis gravitate.*" Compare herewith the law concerning Extreme Unction, can. 940, par. 2.

32. Can. 878, par. 1.

33. Blat, *op. cit.* III, pars. I, p. 224, sq.

34. Can. 897.

35. Canons 401, par. 1, 873, par. 2, 899, par. 2.

36. Can. 899, par. 2.

37. Can. 451, par. 2.

38. Can. 899, par. 3.

39. Cf. Blat, *op. cit.*, p. 268, interprets "*quaevis reservatio*" as referring to the reservations of the *Ordinary* and bases his interpretation on the context of canon 900 and on the Decree of the Holy Office, July 13, 1916. Augustine, *op. cit.*, p. 335, gives the same interpretation. The chapter in which canon 900 appears bears the title "*De reservatione peccatorum.*" The expression "*quaevis reservatio*" is rather broad. The omission of "*Ordinariorum*" from the expression in canon 900 rather than its use in a former decree should be taken into consideration. The reservation of censures is to be taken up in later canons of the Code according to the third paragraph of the introductory canon of the chapter here in question. Hence for the present, the only serious doubt that concerns us in the interpretation of "*quaevis reservatio*" is whether the sin of false accusation "*de crimine sollicitationis,*" reserved to the Holy See, comes under the regulations of canon 900. It is quite difficult to understand how the Code would place this papal reservation in the same class with the reservations of the Ordinary. However, since it is a question of absolution from very grave sin in both kinds of reservations, part of canon 900 seems applicable to the sin reserved in canon 894. And it is improbable that the lawgiver would demand a more urgent reason for considering the reservation as having ceased merely because the Superior to whom the sin is reserved is of higher standing. If we consider the question of absolution from censures in more urgent cases, we find that the same reasons hold good for absolving from any and all kinds of censures *latae sententiae*, "*quoquo modo reservatis*" Cf. The Eccl. Review, Jan. 1919, article by Gearin, p. 67.

40. Blat, *op. cit.* III, par. I, p. 237: *relativa, quia—sacramentalis jurisdictio habita non aufertur nisi quodam in casu peccati* et quoad determinatum personam.

41. Feb. 8, 1745.

42. The constitution of Benedict XIV called *Apostolici muneris*, Feb. 8, 1745, is an explicit declaration of the meaning which the lawgiver intended to convey by the terms he used in the *Sacramentum Poenitentiae*, and a solution of certain doubts concerning the extent of the law. The terms "*deficiente quocumque alio sacerdote, qui confessarii munus obire possit,*" are interpreted in the following passage: *sacerdotibus* (*scl. qui rei sunt complicitatis in peccato turpi, etc.*) *ita interdici . . absolvere, ut si alius aliquis sacerdos non defuerit, etiamsi forte iste alius simplex tantummodo sacerdos fuerit, sive alias ad confessiones audiendas non approbatus, possit nihilominus ipse sacerdos simplex confessionem excipere et absolutionem impertire.* In the third paragraph of the constitution, it is stated that the law of *Sacramentum Poenitentiae* does not extend to cases in which there is danger of "*gravis infamiae vel scandali.*" Moreover, if the guilty confessor construes such a case as the one just mentioned or purposely neglects to prevent the danger implied, the absolution is valid but illicit, and he incurs the censure attached to the transgression. Thus the fourth paragraph.

The constitution *Convocatis*, Nov. 25, 1749, n. XXIII contains the monitum for confessors in the year of the Jubilee that the faculty *absolvendi complicem* is not included in their otherwise ample powers.

The encyclical *Inter praeteritos*, Dec. 3, 1749, par. 56, sqq. refers to the monitum of Convocatis and summarizes the law concerning the *absolutio complicis* as given in *Sacramentum Poenitentiae* and explained in *Apostolici muneris.*

The encyclical *Benedictus Deus*, Dec. 25, 1750, an extension of the Jubilee to the whole Catholic world, excludes (par. 5) the faculty *absolvendi complicem* from its generous grant of powers.

The constitution of Pius IX *Apostolicae Sedis*, Oct. 12, 1869, par. 1, n. X, repeats substantially the penal sanction established by Benedict XIV.

43. Cf. Morino, *Theol. Mor.*, II, p. 374, footnote 1.

44. Canon 16, par. 1, could be cited in support of this contention.

45. E. g. *Sacramentum Poenitentiae*, par. 4: *Demum magnopere cupientes a sacerdotalis iudicii, et sacri tribunalis sanctitate omnem turpitudinis occasionem, et Sacramentorum contemptum, et Ecclesiae iniuriam longe submovere, et tam exitiosa huiusmodi mala prorsus eliminare, et quantum in Domino possumus, animarum periculis occurrere, quas sacrilegi quidam, daemonis potius quam Dei ministri, loco eas per Sacramentum Creatori suo ac nostro reconciliandi maiori peccatorum mole onerantes, in profundum iniquitatis barathrum nefarie submergunt, . . . omnibus et singulis sacerdotibus . . . interdicimus et prohibemus, etc.*

46. Can. 2222, par. 2: *Superior . . non solum ius, sed etiam officium habet . . prohibendi clerico exercitium sacri ministerii aut etiam eundem ab officio . . amovendi; quae omnia in casu non habent rationem poenae.*

47. D'Annibale, *Theol. Mor.* III, n. 324; Sebastiani, *Summarium Theol. Mor.* p. 273, ed. 1919. *Salva reverentia*, it must be said that the second argument looks like a *petitio principii.*

48. Cf. Cappello, *De Censuris*, p. 50.

49. *De Censuris*, p. 55.

50. *Ius Poenale*, Trent, 1920, p. 36, footnote 2.

51. *De Delictis et Poenis*, p. 133.

52. *Commentarium in Const. Apost. Sedis*, p. 152.

53. *De Censuris*, p. 33, footnote 1.

54. *Op. cit.* VI, n. 561.

55. Compare Chelodi, *Ius Matrimoniale*, p. 38, who, in his comment on canon 1043, explicitly calls attention to the fact that "*periculum mortis*" is the term applied, and not "*articulus mortis.*"

56. *Si praedictae infamiae, aut scandali pericula sibi ultro ipse confingat, ubi non sunt*: *Apostolici muneris*, par. 3.

57. Cf. Morino, *Theol. Mor.* II, p. 377, footnote 3.

58. Thus Putzer, *Comment. in Facult. Apost.*, p. 348; Morino, *op cit., loc. cit.*

59. Cf. Blat, *op. cit.* III, par. I, ed. 1920, p. 260, Noldin, *op cit.*, p. 429.

60. Blat, *loc. cit.*

61. June 1, 1741, par. 3.

62. May 36, 1742, par. IX, n. V.

63. Feb. 8, 1745, par. 2.

64. Can. 7.

65. Can. 258, par. 1.

66. *Const. cit.*, par. 1.

67. *Const. cit.*, par. 3.

68. *Op. cit.* III, par. I, p. 260, ed. 1920.

69. Cappello, *De Censuris*, p. 97.

70. Blat, *op. cit.*, p. 261, thinks that the sin is reserved once the accuser has complied with canon 1936: *Denuntiatio scriptis a denuntiante subsignatis vel oretenus fieri debet loci Ordinario, vel cancellario Curiae vel vicariis foraneis vel parochis, a quibus tamen, si viva voce facta fuerit, scriptis est consignanda et statim ad Ordinarium deferenda,* though the accuser failed in carrying out the prescript of canon 1937: *Qui delictum denuntiat debet promotori iustitiae adiumenta suppeditare ad eiusdem delicti probationem.* Blat considers the formal distinction between the

sin reserved "*ratione sui*" and the sin censured in canon 2363 as founded in "*crimen illud 'apud iudicem ecclesiasticum' qua talem deferre.*"

71. *De Delictis et Poenis*, p. 344.

72. *De Censuris*, p. 97.

73. Can. 1936.

74. *Commentarium Codicis Iuris Canonici, Lib. IV, De Processibus*, pp. 504, 531.

75. True enough, the crimes that come up for the judicial procedure in Title XIX, Book IV of the Code are of a public nature. Granted that solicitation were always a *delictum occultum*, the terms used for the procedure against public crimes could be and are most appropriately applied in the procedure against occult crimes. Noval, *op. cit.*, p. 503, adduces the crime of solicitation as an applicable instance of one of the prescripts of canon 1935, par. 2.

76. Sole, *De Delictis et Poenis*, p. 346, interprets the phrase "*firmo praescripto can.* 894" as an instance in which the Code has made an express provision contrary to the law concerning the cessation of censure and sin in canon 2246, par. 3. That interpretation is hardly acceptable in view of the fact that in canon 2246, par. 3, neither a general (*e. g. nisi aliud iure expresse caveatur*) nor a particular (*e. g. salvo praescripto can.* 2363) allowance is made for an exception to the contrary, which provision could be justifiably expected because of the manner in which the law is expressed: *reservatio peccati penitus cessat*, not to speak of the consistency of the Code in its use of provisional phrases or clauses in connection with prescripts especially of a general nature, such as is the prescript of canon 2246, par. 6, on the cessation of censure and sin.

77. Cf. canon 2228: *Poena lege statuta non incurritur, nisi delictum fuerit in suo genere perfectum secundum proprietatem verborum legis.*

78. Cf. Slater, The Ecclesiastical Review, November, 1918, pp. 458, sqq. Gearin, The Ecclesiastical Review, January, 1919, pp. 61, sqq. A writer, H. A. J. ibid., p. 69, sq.

79. Canon 899, par. 1, seems to favor somewhat the opinion, that ignorance excuses from the reservation of sin: *curent locorum Ordinarii ut ad subditorum notitiam quo meliore eis videatur modo eaedem* (*scl. reservationes*) *deducantur*—Cf. Cappello, *De Censuris*, p. 99; Sabetti-Barrett, *Comp. Theol. Mor.*, 27th ed., 1919, p. 752, sq.; Sebastiani, *Summarium Theol. Mor.* 3d ed. 1919, Turin, p. 269, sq.

80. *Op. cit.* III, par. I, ed. 1920, p. 268.

81. The Eccl. Rev., Jan. 1919, p. 67.

82. With regard to matters of conscience, such as have been discussed in the preceding pages, it might be well to remark here that at the beginning of the late war the Cardinal Secretary of State sent a circular letter to the Apostolic Delegates, advising that all letters for the Holy Office and the Sacred Penitentiary be sent in double envelopes, the outer one to be addressed to the Cardinal Secretary of State, the inner one, to the Holy Office or the S. Penitentiary. This method obviously was a better protection for communications that of their very nature demand the greatest privacy. No doubt, in the future, in similar contingencies, the same method will suggest itself as the most practicable. The right to *direct communication* with the Roman Congregations. Offices and Tribunals holds good especially in matters of secrecy and privacy in the realm of conscience.

## X

## FACULTAS REMITTENDI, IN CASIBUS OCCULTIS, POENAS LATAE SENTENTIAE IURE COMMUNI STATUTAS EXCEPTIS CENSURIS SPECIALISSIMO VEL SPECIALI MODO SEDI APOSTOLICAE RESERVATIS

Other restrictions on the ordinary or delegated jurisdiction of hearing confessions, established by the law, are those contained in the reserved censures. Censures that are called *nemini reservatae* place, of course, no restriction on the exercise of jurisdiction in the sacramental forum.[1]

It lies beyond the scope of the present study to enter upon a discussion of the various censures that resrict the jurisdictional power of the confessor. For a thorough understanding of reserved censures, special treatises on that subject would have to be consulted. It is highly desirable that the document of diocesan faculties have the censures listed in a manner, that would facilitate recalling them from time to time. The classification that suggests itself as most helpful is the usual enumeration according to the general divisions and sub-divisions given in text-books, namely: I. Excommunications (A) reserved to the Holy See (a) *specialissimo modo* (b) *speciali modo* (c) *simpliciter;* (B) reserved to the Ordinary (a) by the Code (b) by the Council of Baltimore; (C) *nemini reservatae;* II Interdicts; III Suspensions (A) reserved to the Holy See; (B) reserved to the Ordinary; (C) *nemini reservatae.* Obviously, any censures which the Ordinary has established and reserved to himself may be added in their logical places to the abovementioned classes. The Code prescribes no special procedure for the establishment of reserved censures in the diocese. Canon 895 may be taken as the norm, according to the general prescript of canon 20, since there is no question of the *application* of punishments, but only of their establishment. Canon 2246, par. 1, and most probably, canon 897, prescribe certain preliminary considerations of the procedure of reserving censures. Common law, canon 2253°, n. 1, grants all confessors the right to absolve, in the sacramental forum only, from censures that are not reserved.

The Ordinary may include in the diocesan faculties the delegated jurisdiction to absolve from all or certain censures that are reserved to him.[2] Canon 401, par. 1, grants the *poenitentiarius canonicus* the right to absolve "*a peccatis et a censuris Episcopo reservatis*," which jurisdiction is ordinary.

Canon 2237, par. 2, permits the Ordinary or those whom he delegates,—as he may do in the document of faculties,—to remit in *casus occulti* the punishments *latae sententiae* established by common law. The censures reserved to the Holy See in a special and a most special manner are excepted, and the regulations of canons 2254 and 2290 concerning *casus urgentiores* are not invalidated or impaired by this concession.

Sole[3] interprets "*casus occulti*" as such cases in which the punishments are inflicted because of a "*delictum occultum sive materialiter sive formaliter.*" Can a *delictum* which is only formally occult be called truly occult? It seems doubtful, to say the least, that a crime, the occurrence of which is known, could be called truly occult merely because the imputability has not been established. "*Casus occultus*" seems to imply that the transgression itself is occult, as appears deducible from the definition of *occultum*, which is given as the contradictory of *publicum*.[4]

The canon, just quoted, referring to the absolution particularly from censures in occult cases states expressly that the censures in question are those established by common law.[5] Hence, e. g. the excommunication of the Third Council of Baltimore, n. 124, is not affected by this legislation.[6]

## Absolution From Censures in Danger of Death and in "Casibus Urgentioribus."

The document of faculties need not call attention to the powers concerning absolution from censures granted the confessor by the Code for "*periculum mortis*" and the more urgent cases, since this matter is expressly and extensively legislated in canon 2254.

For the case of danger of death the following canons are to be noted: Can. 882: *In periculo mortis omnes sacerdotes, licet ad confessiones non approbati, valide et licite absolvunt quoslibet poenitentes a quibusvis peccatis aut censuris, quantumvis reservatis et notoriis, etiamsi praesens sit sacerdos approbatus, salvo praescripto can.* 884, 2252.—Can. 2252: *Qui in periculo mortis constituti, a sacerdote, specialis factultatis experte, receperunt absolutionem ab aliqua censura ab homine vel a censura specialissimo modo Sedi Apostolicae reservata, tenentur, postquam convaluerint, obligatione recurrendi, sub poena reincidentiae, ad illum qui censuram tulit, si agatur de censura ab homine; ad S. Poenitentiariam vel ad Episcopum aliumve favultate praeditum, ad normam can.* 2254, *par.* 1, *si de censura a iure; eorumque mandatis parendi.*—Canon 884, referred to above, has been treated at length in another part of this study.—Canon 2252 imposes the obligation of recurring to the authorities there mentioned in two cases only, namely, 1) when the person in danger of death was absolved from a censure "*ab homine,*" i. e. "*si feratur per modum praecepti peculiaris vel per sententiam iudicialem condemnatoriam, etsi in iure statuta;*'"[7] 2) when the person in danger of death was absolved from a censure reserved to the Holy See in a most special manner. After the person in question is removed from the danger of death, the obligation of recurring to the proper authorities holds under penalty of re-incurring the censure from which the penitent was absolved. No time limit is set within which this obligation must be fulfilled, at least not for the case of absolution from a censure *ab homine.* The penitent is obliged to obey the mandates of the respective authorities.

It is to be noted that the canon uses the term "*convaluerint.*" This would refer *per se* only to those who had been in danger of death from sickness or injury. However, the term is to be interpreted as including also those who have been in danger of death from other causes.

The Code itself describes what is meant by *casus urgentiores.* They are such cases in which censures *latae sententiae* cannot be observed exteriorly without grave danger of scandal or loss of good name, or in which the penitent would suffer great mental anguish if the sacramental absolution from his grievous sin were long delayed because of the time needed for the proper procedure on the part of a competent Superior. For this latter case authors[8] suggest that the confessor awaken in the penitent the disposition necessary for a *casus urgentior.*

The confessor may absolve in these more urgent cases from censures *latae sententiae* reserved in any manner, after the obligation is imposed, *iniuncto onere,* of recurring, under penalty of incurring the censure again, within a month at least, to the proper authorities, the S. Poenitentiaria or the bishop or some other Superior who has the required faculty. The recourse to the authorities is to be made "*per epistolam et per confessarium.*" The Code does not specify which confessor is to help the penitent in forwarding the written recourse. Cappello[9] permits the penitent to have immediate personal recourse to the authorities without the intervention of a confessor. That does not seem to be the intention of the law.

The above recourse is to be made *"si id fieri possit sine gravi incommodo,"* which wise provision keeps the obligation both for the penitent and the confessor from becoming an unbearable burden.—When the letter of recourse is sent to the authorities, the name of the penitent should not be mentioned (*"reticito nomine"*). Hence, perhaps the wording of the canon *"per epistolam et per confessarium."* The obligation of observing the mandates of the respective authority binds the penitent, though not evidently under the penalty of re-incurring the censure.

When the recourse is morally impossible, namely, when neither the confessor nor the penitent is able to send the letter and the penitent finds it hard to go to another confessor, or when the penitent does not know how to write and the confessor, who could send the written recourse, will not be able to give the penitent the rescript, then the confessor may absolve the penitent without imposing the burden of recourse. The one exception to this exception is the case in which the penitent has been absolved from the censure inflicted by canon 2367.—If absolution is granted without the obligation or recourse the confessor is to impose the obligations required by law, natural and positive, an appropriate penance and a satisfaction for the censure.[10] Unless the penitent fulfills these obligations within the time prescribed by the confessor the censure again becomes effective.

After the absolution granted in *casu urgentiori* by a confessor who did not have the special faculty required for the censure, the penitent is free to go to a confessor, who has the required faculty, to obtain absolution.[11] In this instance the penitent is to observe the mandates of the confessor. The obligation to fulfill the prescripts of the Superior, imposed on the occasion of the recourse after the former absolution, ceases upn receiving absolution from a confessor who possesses the necessary faculty. The law evidently implies that the privilege of can. 2254, par. 2, cannot be used after the mandates of the Superior have arrived. Hence, it is not permissible to discard the mandates of the Superior in the hope of finding an easier penance.

In order to obtain absolution according to the norm of canon 2254, par. 2, the penitent is obliged to confess at least the sin for which the censure was inflicted, since it would be impossible for the confessor to judge the case and give the proper mandates.[12]

## Notes

### X

1. Can. 2253, n. 1.
2. Can. 2253, n. 3.
3. *Op. cit.*, page 99.
4. Can. 2197, nn. 1, 4.
5. Kinane, The Irish Eccl. Record, Nov. 1917, page 378, defends the view that canon 6, n. 5, does not include punishments imposed by particular laws. This view is based on the purpose of canon 6 and on the context of the provisions of that canon. The view defended by Kinane is almost beyond a doubt the only tenable one on this point.
6. Conc. Plen. Balt. III, n. 124: . . . *poenam excommunicationis statuimus, Ordinario reservatam, ipso facto incurrendam ab eis, qui postquam divortium civile obtinuerint, matrimonium ausi fuerint attentare.*
7. Can. 2217, par. 1, n. 3.
8. Arregui, *Summarium Theol. Mor.*, page 406.
9. *Op. cit.*, page 34, footnote 6.
10. Hence, a double penance, one for the sins confessed and one for the censure incurred.
11. Why the expression "*consequatur absolutionem*" is used here, can. 2254, par. 2, is a matter of speculation. The penitent has been absolved from the censure in the former confession, which absolution was direct. Cf. S. C. S. Off., Aug. 19, 1891, ad 3; March 30, 1892, ad 6. The term could mean the absolution "*in actu primo*" as it is given in the case of sins already remitted. Cr. S. Alph., *Theol. Mor.*, VI, n. 427. From the tenor of the paragraph in which the expression occurs, it appears to mean the absolution from the obligations imposed by the confessor according to can. 2254, par. 1.
12. The whole canon reads as follows: Par. 1. *In casibus urgentioribus, si nempe censurae latae sententiae exterius servari nequeant sine periculo gravis scandali vel infamiae, aut si durum sit poenitenti in statu gravis peccati permanere per tempus necessarium ut Superior competens*

*provideat, tunc quilibet confessarius in foro sacramentali ab eisdem, quoquo modo reservatis, absolvere potest, iniuncto onere recurrendi, sub poena reincidentiae, intra mensem saltem per epistolam et per confessarium, si id fieri possit sine gravi incommodo, reticito nomine, ad. S. Poenitentiariam vel ad Episcopum aliumve Superiorem praeditum facultate et standi eius mandatis.*

Par. 2. *Nihil impedit quominus poenitens, etiam post acceptam, ut supra, absolutionem, facto quoque recursu ad Superiorem, alium adeat confessarium facultate praeditum, ab eoque, repetita confessione saltem delicti sum censura, consequatur absolutionem; qua obtenta, mandata ab eodem accipiat, quin teneatur postea stare aliis mandatis ex parte Superioris supervenientibus.*

Par. 3. *Quod si in casu aliquo extraordinario hic recursus sit moraliter impossibilis, tunc ipsemet confessarius, excepto casu quo agatur de absolutione censurae de qua in can. 2367, potest absolutionem concedere sine onere de quo supra, iniunctis tamen de iure iniungendis, et imposita congrua poenitentia et satisfactione pro censura, ita ut poenitens, nisi intra congruum tempus a confessario praefiniendum poenitentiam egerit ac satisfactionem dederit, recidat in censuram.*

## XI

## FACULTAS ABSOLVENDI AB HAERESI, SCHISMATE ET APOSTASIA, PRAEVIA ABIURATIONE IURIDICE PERACTA, ET ABSOLUTIONE IN FORO EXTERNO ACCEPTA

The document of diocesan faculties could direct the attention of the confessors to a power granted in canon 2314, par. 2. According to that concession, any confessor may absolve apostates, heretics and schismatics in the forum of conscience, once they have made the juridical abjuration and received absolution from the local Ordinary in the exterior forum. The Vicar General cannot absolve the penitent in question in the exterior forum without a special mandate from the bishop. The juridical element of the abjuration consists in the presence of the local Ordinary or his delegate and at least two witnesses. If the crime of apostasy, heresy or schism has not been brought to the external forum, the absolution from the excommunication in the internal forum is reserved to the Holy See in a special manner.[1] It might be of some value to add here a few remarks concerning this excommunication.—Atheists, pantheists, free thinkers and all whose systems of philosophy or theology are incompatible with the christian religion are to be reckoned among the apostates.[2] Spiritistic experiments imply heresy, and cause the offender to incur the censure of canon 2314, par. 2.[3] The question whether a heretic incurs the censure only then when he becomes a member of a non-catholic denomination is settled in the negative by the definition in canon 1325, par. 2, and by canon 2314, par. 1, n. 3.

## Notes

### XI

1. Canon 2314, par. 1: *Omnes a christiana fide apostatae et omnes et singuli haeretici aut schismatici:* 1. *Incurrunt ipso facto excommunicationem;*—par. 2. *Absolutio ab excommunicatione de qua in par.* 1, *in foro conscientiae impertienda, est speciali modo Sedi Apostolicae reservata. Si tamen delictum apostasiae, haeresis vel schismatis ad forum externum Ordinarii loci quovis modo deductum fuerit, etiam per voluntariam confessionem, idem Ordinarius, non vero Vicarius Generalis sine mandato speciali, resipiscentem, praevia abiuratione iuridice peracta aliisque servatis de iure servandis, sua auctoritate ordinaria in foro exteriore absolvere potest; ita vero absolutus, potest deinde a peccato absolvi a quolibet confessario in foro conscientiae. Abiuratio vero habetur iuridice peracta cum fit coram ipso Ordinario loci vel eius delegato et saltem duobus testibus.* The definition of the above mentioned crimes is given in canon 1325, par. 2; *Post receptum baptismum si quis, nomen retinens christianum, pertinaciter aliquam ex veritatibus fide divina et catholica credendis denegat aut de ea dubitat, haereticus; si a christiana totaliter recedit, apostata; si denique subesse renuit Summo Pontifici aut cum membris Ecclesiae ei subiectis communicare recusat, schismaticus est.*

2. Cf. Capello, *op. cit.*, page 65.

3. Cf. Chelodi, *Ius Poenale*, p. 62.

## XII

## FACULTAS (DATA PAROCHO ALIIVE SACERDOTI QUI INFIRMIS ASSISTAT) CONCEDENDI INFIRMIS BENEDICTIONEM APOSTOLICAM CUM INDULGENTIA PLENARIA IN ARTICULO MORTIS, SECUNDAM FORMAM A PROBATIS LITURGICIS LIBRIS TRADITAM

The priest who assists the sick may now, by common law,[1] grant the apostolic blessing with the plenary indulgence for the hour of death. Formerly this faculty was granted by special concession.[2] The various conditions under which this indulgence is to be gained are usually summed up in text-books of moral theology.[3] Of importance is the requisite mentioned expressly by the Code, namely, that the proper formula be used. If the blessing follows immediately after Extreme Unction, it is not necessary to repeat "*Pax huic domui, etc.*," nor the "*Asperges, etc.*" The priest begins with the "*Adiutorium nostrum, etc.*," and the "*Confiteor, etc.*," must be repeated, though it has been said in the administration both of the Viaticum and Extreme Unction.[4] The Code reminds the priest of the obligation of giving the last blessing: *quam benedictionem impertiri ne omittat.*[5]

### Notes

#### XII

1. Canon 468, par. 2.
2. Cf. Putzer, *Comment. in Facultates Apostolicas,* p. 255.
3. Cf. e. g. Sabetti-Barrett, *Compend. Theol. Mor.,* ed. 27, p. 1085, sq.
4. Putzer, *op. cit.,* page 257.
5. Canon 468, par. 2.

## XIII

1) Facultas dispensandi, urgente mortis periculo, ad consulendum conscientiae et, si casus ferat, legitimationi prolis, tum super forma in matrimonii celebratione servanda, tum super omnibus et singulis impedimentis iuris ecclesiastici, sive publicis sive occultis, etiam multiplicibus, exceptis impedimentis provenientibus ex sacro presbyteratus ordine et ex affinitate in linea recta, consummato matrimonio, remoto scandalo, et in casu disparitatis cultus aut mixtae religionis, praestitis consuetis cautionibus.

2) Facultas dispensandi, in casibus occultis, in quibus ne loci quidem Ordinarius adiri possit, vel nonnisi cum periculo violationis secreti, super omnibus impedimentis exceptis duobus, ut supra, sub clausulis in fine praecedentis facultatis statutis, quoties impedimentum detegatur, cum iam omnia sunt parata ad nuptias, nec matrimonium sine probabili gravis mali periculo differi possit, usquedum dispensatio obtineatur.

3) Eadem facultas valet pro convalidatione matrimonii iam contracti, si idem periculum sit in mora nec tempus suppetat recurrendi ad obtinendam dispensationem.

One of the most important faculties mentioned in the Code is that referring to marriage dispensations in danger of death and in urgent cases. This faculty is treated explicitly in canons 1043, 1044, 1045, 1046. An extensive reference in the document of diocesan faculties to the concessions granted in this matter by the Code would no doubt be of great value to the parish priest.

The faculty granted the local Ordinaries in canon 1043[1] is extended in canon 1044, for cases in which not even the local Ordinary can be reached, to the parish priest, to the priest who assists at the marriage according to the norm of canon 1098, n. 2, and to the confessor for the internal forum in the act of sacramental confession only.[2] Canon 1045 permits the local Ordinaries to use the faculty of canon 1043 as to the dispensation from impediments also outside the danger of death, namely, in certain *casus perplexi.* The same canon grants this faculty, for the *casus perplexi,* to the parish priest, to the priest assisting at a marriage according to the norm of canon 1098, n. 2, and to the confessor; however this concession holds only for occult cases, in which not even the local Ordinary can be reached, or if so, not without danger of violating a secret.

The faculty of canon 1043 may be used *"urgente mortis periculo."* This expression is qualified in the *Litt. Encycl.* S. C. S. Officii, Feb. 20, 1888, as meaning: *quando tempus non suppetit recurrendi ad S. Sedem.* In the document just mentioned the expression *"in gravissimo mortis periculo"* is given the same broad interpretation in connection with the term *"aegroti,"* which goes to show that the concession granted is not to be understood in too literal a sense. The Code does not restrict *"periculum mortis"* to danger arising from sickness. Hence, danger of death from any cause would justify the use of the faculty. It is not of importance whether the *person directly affected* is in danger of death or not.[3]

The prerequisite condition for the use of the faculty is given as *"ad consulendum conscientiae et, si casus ferat, legitimationi prolis."* The Code does not state that the dispensation may be granted *"ex iusta et rationabili causa"* and leave the matter to the decision of the bishop or priest, but legislates expressly that the purpose for which the dispensation is to be granted is to soothe the conscience and to legitimatize the offspring. These motives for granting the dispensation are implicitly declared just and reasonable by the lawgiver.

Apparently the lawgiver excludes other reasons, as for instance to satisfy or quiet bothersome relatives of the persons in question. It would hardly be possible to consider such a motive a just and reasonable cause. Without a just and reasonable cause the dispensation granted by a person inferior to the lawgiver in authority is not only illicit but also invalid.[4] *Salvo meliori iudicio,* the prerequisite motives are essentially necessary for the validity of the dispensation because of the prominence and weight given them in the legislation upon which the present canon is founded.[5]

The *form,* to be observed in the celebration of marriage according to Lib. III, Tit. VII, Cap. VI of the Code may, under the given conditions, be dispensed with. It is to be noted that the Code mentions the form separately from the impediments. The form is likewise treated in its own separate chapter in the Code. It is now apparently a settled matter that form does not constitute an impediment in the present terminology of the Code.[6]

The presence of witnesses, therefore, is not required for the celebration of marriage *"urgente mortis periculo."* If one witness were to be had, there surely would be no obligation to ask him or her to be present for the marriage, since the presence of one witness would not meet the law of the Church on form. However, if two witnesses could be called in, the question immediately arises as to the obligation of observing the form prescribed. Canon 1043 does not specify or indicate, even in a general way, the conditions under which the dispensation may be granted, except those implied by *"urgente mortis periculo," "remoto scandalo,"* and *"praestitis consuetis cautionibus."* These conditions throw no light on the question proposed. From the absence of other requisite conditions it would seem that the lawgiver wished to grant the most liberal interpretation of the applicability of dispensation as to form in danger of death. If the presence of witnesses were a seriously disagreeable matter in such a case, the law concerning the observance of the prescribed form should not be considered binding.

In the case in which the witnesses could be called in *"sine gravi incommodo"* for the persons affected by the dispensation—including the offspring to be legitimatized—the legislation of the Code concerning the convalidation of marriage would have to be followed, provided, of course, that it were a question of simple convalidation. In the supposition that the persons concerned had not attempted marriage and *"urgente periculo mortis"* desired to enter upon marriage, the law concerning form should be observed if it can be done so *"sine gravi incommodo."* This opinion about the observance of the law concerning form, *"sine gravi incommodo,"* in danger of death is stated here merely tentatively. The danger of death which would permit the observance of form does not seem to be a sufficiently just and reasonable cause for dispensing from the observance of form. The expression *"urgente mortis periculo"* is interpreted as referring to such cases in which there is not time enough to have recourse for the dispensations needed. The question of recourse for a dispensation does not enter in the case in which the form could be observed *"sine gravi incommodo.''*—However, since the lawgiver has made no distinction, the necessity of a distinction is not evident.

All impediments of ecclesiastical law with the exception of two, are subject to the power granted in canon 1043. The concession comprehends both public and occult impediments.[7] Even multiple impediments are included.[8] Consanguinity, affinity and crime can be multiple impediments. Whether public honesty and spiritual relationship can be multiple impediments is not certain.[9]

The first exception is the impediment arising from the sacred order of the priesthood. This exception was likewise contained in the decree of the Holy Office, Feb. 20, 1888. Sub-deaconship and deaconship do not limit, therefore, the concession of canon 1043. The second exception is affinity in the direct line, after the marriage has been consummated. The exception refers most probably to all degrees in the direct line.[10] The Church never dispenses in the first degree of affinity *''ex copula licita''* in the direct line.[11] Avanzini[12] states that the Church does not dispense in the other degrees of the direct line either. The reason for this latter fact is not evident. Gasparri suggests the rarity of the occurrence.[13] Of almost exclusively theoretical value is the question whether *consanguinity* in degrees that are certainly of ecclesiastical but only doubtfully of natural law is included in the concession of canon 1043. A negative reply seems deducible from canon 1076, par. 3: *Nunquam matrimonium permittatur, si quod subsit dubium num partes sint consanguineae in aliquo gradu lineae rectae aut in primo gradu lineae collateralis.*

The subjects who may receive the benefit of the concession in canon 1043 are *''subditi proprii ubique commorantes''* because, according to Blat[14], the application of this concession is an act of *potestas iurisdictionis voluntaria.* How this reason would be applicable in the case when the concession is used by the parish priest, the priest assisting a marriage according to canon 1098, n. 2, or the confessor of canon 1044 is not apparent. Most probably the reason for the express reference to the *"proprii subditi ubique commorantes"* in connection with a matter in which its omission would be readily understood because of the applicability of the general principles governing the *potestas iurisdictionis voluntaria*[15] is to be found in the desire of the lawgiver to settle the doubts that could arise concerning the jurisdiction of the parish priest, who, according to canon 1044, enjoys the faculty of canon 1043 as far as his subjects are concerned. The concession may be used likewise to all who are *"actu degentes in proprio territorio."* This could be deduced from the general principles concerning the exercise of voluntary jurisdiction. The term *degentes* is used to include others who are in *in periculo mortis* besides the sick. The term *"actu"* annuls even the requirement of *commoratio menstrua.*

The condition, *"remoto scandalo,"* must be verified at least for the licit granting of the faculty of canon 1043. The terminological setting of the decree of the Holy Office, Feb. 20, 1888, does not permit the condition of removing scandal to be considered as a requisite for the validity of the dispensation. The decree stresses the scandal which could arise from a dispensation granted to persons who have received sub-deaconship or deaconship, or who have made the solemn profession. The absence of any restricting qualification of this condition in the present legislation indicates that the condition is to be verified in all dispensations in which there is question of scandal.

The last phrase of canon 1043, relating to the cautions to be exacted in the cases of disparity of worship and mixed religion, has given rise to serious doubt as to whether the cautions are required for the validity or only for the licitness of the dispensations in question. From the discussion the conclusion seems justifiably deducible:

It is not certain that the cautions are required for the validity. Chelodi[16] sums up the result of the discussion in the careful words: *"his (cautionibus) non requisitis aut denegatis dispensatio non certo valida est."*

As above indicated in considering the obligation of observing the prescribed form *"urgente mortis periculo,"* the powers of canon 1043 cover both *"matrimonium convalidandum"* and *"matrimonium contrahendum."* But the canon does not grant the faculty *"sanandi in radice,"* not only because the *"sanatio in radice"* is reserved to the Holy See,[17] but also because canon 1043 does not include the dispensation from the law *"de renovando consensu"* nor the *"retrotractio circa effectus canonicos ad praeteritum."*

The concession of canon 1043 is made expressly to the local Ordinaries. Canon 1044, however, extends the concession for the cases, in which the local Ordinary cannot be reached, to other ecclesiastical persons. The first person mentioned is the *"parochus."* The term *"parochus"* is to be interpreted according to canon 451.

In the supposition that curates or assistants are not *"vicarii paroeciales plena potestate paroeciali praediti,"* the question arises whether the parish priest by virtue of canon 1044 has ordinary jurisdiction for the cases there mentioned, and can consequently delegate the curate or assistant for such cases.[18] The doubt originates in the consideration that ordinary jurisdiction is by law attached to an office, and that in canon 1044 the parish priest is classified with other ecclesiastics who need have no office. Vlaming[19] replies negatively to the above question: *Sunt nonnisi delegatae (scl. facultates in cann.* 1044 *et* 1045, *par.* 3), *ideoque non possunt subdelegari.* The reason he gives is that there is no office to which the ordinary jurisdiction, to be exercised in the external forum, could be attached. This reason would hold for the *"sacerdos"* of canon 1044, if the term *officium* is to be interpreted strictly for this canon. However, the context of the canon warrants a broad interpretation of the term *officium* and hence, ordinary jurisdiction could be attached to the "*munus spirituale.*"[20] From this viewpoint, Vlaming's argument would likewise not hold for the case of the parish priest. Granted, that the jurisdiction in question is delegated, it would be difficult to prove that it could not be sub-delegated, since the powers of canon 1044 are granted by the Holy See.[21] De Smet[22] claims that the parish priest, the simple priest and the confessor have *iurisdictio ordinaria vicaria* for the cases of canons 1044 and 1045.[23] The reason this author implies is that the priests mentioned have a "*munus*" and to it is attached, by law, the *facultas dispensandi.* This reason seems admissible according to the broad interpretation of *officium.* The Code permits the delegation of ordinary jurisdiction, whether it be proper or vicarious.[24] Chelodi[25] says that there can hardly be any doubt that the delegate of the parish priest has the same faculty of canons 1044 and 1045, "*attento canone* 200 *par.* 1, *et resp. C. S.* 29 *iul.,* 1910." This author presupposes that the jurisdiction of the parish priest is "*ordinaria.*"

The practical solution of the difficulty is to grant the assistants or curates the necessary powers in the document of diocesan faculties. If this is not done, the parish priest could follow the norm of canon 209 concerning the "*dubium iuris.*"

The other priests concerned in canon 1044 have been mentioned in the course of the above discussion on the nature of the jurisdiction granted in canon 1044, namely, the priest who assists at a marriage according to canon 1908, par. 2, and the confessor. The latter enjoys the faculty in a limited sense only. His power in this matter may be exercised in the internal forum in the act of sacramental confession only. Hence, only occult impediments come under his jurisdiction for the internal sacramental forum.[26]

The faculty of canon 1044 cannot be applied if the Ordinary can be reached. If the priest cannot come in contact with the Ordinary, that is with the bishop of the diocese, the vicar general, or "sede vacante" the administrator, by letter or in person in sufficient time to receive a dispensation, there is no obligation of having recourse.

The telegraph or the telephone may be used in very rare instances but there is no obligation to resort to these methods of communication.[27] In fact, it is forbidden "*ex regula ordinaria*" to use these methods for any dispensation. The letter of the Secretary of State to the Bishops of Italy, Dec. 10, 1891, is to the point: *Attentis incommodis, quae iam acciderunt et denuo facile evenire possunt in excipiendis gratiarum petitionibus transmissis per telegraphum, Sanctitas Sua praescripsit, ne deinceps, ex regula ordinaria, ulla S. Congregatio . . . eiusmodi preces medio memorato exhibitas admittat. Quum eadem rationes quoad Curias episcopales etiam valeant, Sanctitas Sua vult ut Pastores Dioecesani quoque se ad hanc praescriptionem conforment.*[28] Even the validity of a dispensation may be endangered by the methods under consideration, especially in those cases in which many points are to be expressed "*de validitate.*"

*Salvo meliori iudicio,* there is no obligation to have recourse to a person delegated by the Ordinary. It seems to be beyond the jurisdiction of the Ordinary to make the recourse for the faculty of canon 1043 obligatory, because the power granted in canon 1044 is given by the highest lawgiver, whose authority overrules that of inferiors. Vlaming[28a] holds that the parish priest (and other priests mentioned in canon 1044) would dispense invalidly if he would not apply to the ecclesiastic delegated by the Ordinary, in the case where there would be enough time to apply to the delegated person, but not enough time to have recourse to the Ordinary.

It is expressly legislated that the faculty of canon 1044 can be used only in danger of death and for the purpose of peace of conscience and, if required, of legitimatizing the offspring. The removal of scandal and the subscribing to the usual cautions are conditions of the dispensations and cannot be considered as coming under the head of "*iisdem rerum adiunctis.*"

The faculty granted the local Ordinaries for danger of death is extended by canon 1045, paragraphs 1 and 2, with certain limitations, to other perplexing cases. This canon requires in the first place that the conditional clauses at the end of canon 1043 be observed; namely, concerning the removal of scandal and the subscribing to the usual cautions. The question as to whether the requirement of the cautions is *ad validitatem* takes on a different aspect in this canon, because, generally speaking, the cases there mentioned are not so urgent as the case of danger of death. In those cases in which the imminent evil is, according to common estimation, as serious as death itself, there seems to be no reason why the milder opinion on the requirement of the cautions could not be consistently upheld. In other cases, namely, those that are not so urgent, it would seem unjustifiable to interpret the mind of the lawgiver according to the milder view, at least as long as there is no definite or indicative official pronouncement on the matter.

The faculty of dispensing covers the impediments of canon 1043. Of course, the impediments arising from the sacred order of priesthood and from affinity in the direct line after the consummation of marriage, are excepted. No mention whatsoever of form is made as is in canon 1043. Consistently with his classification of form among the diriment impediments, De Smet[29] writes: *non videtur ex hac omissione concludendum ad illius exclusionem ab ambitu facultatis.... Ad minus probabile est canone* 1045 *comprehendi clandestinitatem, adeoque, attento can.* 15, *practice certum est.* Other authors[30] state expressly and unqualifiedly that form is not included among the dispensable impediments of canon 1045.[31]

The perplexing case mentioned in the first paragraph of canon 1045 is that in which an impediment, obviously a dispensable one, is discovered, "*detegatur,*" after everything is ready for the marriage, and the marriage cannot be deferred, without the probable danger of a serious evil, until a dispensation can be obtained from the Holy See.

It is not required for the legitimate exercise of the powers granted in canon 1045 that the impediment be altogether unknown up to the time of the marriage, but it suffices if the bishop, or the priest[32] does not know of the existence of the impediment.[33]

The clause "*cum iam omnia sunt parata ad nuptias*" is, as are also other clauses of canon 1045, to be interpreted "*moraliter, scrupulis abdicatis.*"[34] The condition expressed by this clause does not suffice, of itself, to allow the use of the dispensatory power under consideration. Another condition is required, namely, that the marriage cannot be postponed long enough to obtain a dispensation from the Holy See. The impossibility of postponing the marriage celebration must arise, not from some arbitrary source, but from a probable danger of some serious evil, "*malum.*" It matters not of what nature this evil is. It is to be noted that the Code here speaks of recourse to the Holy See. Hence, the faculty could be used even though some ecclesiastical person enjoying the faculty by delegation from the Holy See could be reached.[35]

The first paragraph of canon 1045 refers to the use of the faculty in the case of "*matrimonii contrahendi.*" The second paragraph extends the applicability of the faculty to the convalidation of a marriage that has been contracted invalidly because of any of the impediments that are covered by the faculty. It is question here only of the simple convalidation,[36] since convalidation by means of "*sanatio in radice*" is not included in the faculty.[37] The conditions "*probabile periculum gravis mali in mora*" and insufficient time for recourse to the Holy See are requisites for the use of the faculty.

The third paragraph permits the priests mentioned in canon 1044, namely, the parish priest, the simple priest who assists at a marriage according to canon 1098, n. 2, and the confessor, to use this faculty for marriages to be contracted or already contracted under the same conditions and circumstances in which the Ordinaries may use it, with this restriction, however, that the cases must be occult and such that is impossible to reach the local Ordinary or, if it be possible to reach him, not without the danger of violating a secret.

For a proper understanding of an *occult case* in connection with marriage impediments, it is sufficient to refer to the possibility that a case may still be occult though the impediment be public. The Code has given no definition of "occult" or "public" case. Hence the former interpretation still holds in this matter.[38]

It is to be noted that when there is danger, in applying to the Ordinary, of the violation of a secret, sacramental or extra-sacramental, the faculty here under discussion obtains. If this danger be present in the recourse to the local bishop but not in that to the vicar general, or vice versa, there is, *salvo meliori iudicio,* an obligation of having recourse to that Ordinary, whose granting of the required faculties would not endanger the secret.

The Code legislates that the parish priest and the priest who assists at a marriage according to canon 1098, n. 2, are to notify the local Ordinary immediately of the dispensation granted for the external forum, and that note of the dispensation be made in the "*liber matrimoniorum.*"[39] This prescript of the Code refers apparently to all dispensations for the external forum that are granted in danger of death and in urgent cases.[40]

As to the obligation of making note of the dispensation in the matrimonial register, there is no doubt that it rests on the parish priest in the instances in which he assists. In the cases, however, in which the priest assists according to canon 1098, n. 2, it is difficult to say on whom precisely the obligation rests. If canon 1103, par. 3, may be taken as a norm, the obligation would rest primarily on the priest. Perhaps the Curia would ultimately have the burden of informing the respective parish priest of the dispensation, with the purpose of having him note it down in the matrimonial register. Whether there is any obligation of informing the local Ordinary of the dispensation granted and of noting same in the matrimonial register in the cases in which there is danger of violation of a secret, depends upon the nature and the circumstances of the individual case.

## Notes

### XIII

1. *Urgente mortis periculo, locorum Ordinarii, ad consulendum conscientiae et, si casus ferat, legitimationi prolis, possunt tum super forma in matrimonii celebratione servanda, tum super omnibus et singulis impedimentis juris ecclesiastici, sive publicis sive occultis, etiam multiplicibus, exceptis impedimentis provenientibus ex sacro presbyteratus ordine et ex affinitate in linea recta, consummato matrimonio, dispensare proprios subditos ubique commorantes et omnes in proprio territorio actu degentes, remoto scandalo, et, si dispensatio concedatur super cultus disparitate aut mixta religione, praestitis consuetis cautionibus.*

2. Can. 1044: *In eisdem rerum adiunctis de quibus in can.* 1043, *et solum pro casibus in quibus ne loci quidem Ordinarius adiri possit, eadem dispensandi facultate pollet tum parochus, tum sacerdos qui matrimonio, ad normam can.* 1098, *n.* 2, *assistit, tum confessarius, sed hic pro foro interno in actu sacramentalis confessionis tantum.* Can. 1098: *Si haberi vel adiri nequeat sine gravi incommodo parochus vel Ordinarius vel sacerdos delegatus qui matrimonio assistant ad normam canonum* 1095, 1096: 1. *In mortis periculo validum et licitum est matrimonium contractum coram solis testibus; et etiam extra mortis periculum, dummodo prudenter provideatur eam rerum conditionem esse per mensem duraturam;* 2. *In utroque casu, si praesto sit alius sacerdos qui adesse possit, vocari et, una cum testibus, matrimonio assistere debet, salva coniugii validitate coram solis testibus.*

3. S. Cong. S. Off., July 1, 1891—Cf. Sebastiani, *op. cit.*, page 333; De Smet, *De Sponsalibus et Matrim.*, II, 3rd ed., page 126.

4. Can. 84, par. 1.

5. S. C. S. Off., Feb. 20, 1888: *ut morituri in tanta temporis angustia in faciem Ecclesiae rite copulari, et propriae conscientiae consulere valeant.*

6. Thus Vlaming, *Praelectiones Iuris Matrimonii*, I, 3rd ed., page

155, sq.: *Terminologia Codicis—quam aliqui recentiores canonistae iampri dem usurpaverunt—nomine "impedimenti" nonnisi id accipit quod ex parte ipsius personae contrahentis matrimonii sive solam liceitatem impedit sive etiam validitatem. Quae vero ex parte consensus aut non observatae legitimae formae matrimonio valide ac licite ineundo obstare possunt, ea Codex canonibus suis de impedimentis non comprehendit, sed seorsum moderatur.* Reference could further be made to the chapter of the Code on the convalidation of marriage, in which the distinction between impediments and form is consistently and sharply drawn.

7. Can. 1037.

8. Chelodi, *Ius Matrimoniale,* pp. 98, 100, 108, 111, 114.

9. Cf. Chelodi, *op. cit.,* pp. 111, 114; De Smet, *op. cit.* II, page 134, footnote 3, page 137; Vlaming, *op. cit.,* pp. 343, 365.

10. Can. 1077, par. 1.

11. Gasparri, *De Matrimonio,* II, page 566.

12. *Acta S. Sedis,* II, p. 127.

13. Cf. De Smet, *op. cit.* II, page 129; Wernz, *Ius Decretalium,* IV, par. 2, page 295.

14. *Op. cit.,* par. I, page 544.

15. Can. 201, par. 2.

16. *Ius Matrim.,* page 38.

17. De Smet, *op. cit.,* II, page 217.

18. Chelodi, *Ius Matrim.,* page 43.

19. *Op. cit.* II, page 37.

20. Cf. canons 145 and 197. The Code does not require an "*officium ecclesiasticum stricto sensu acceptum*" as a prerequisite for ordinary jurisdiction.

21. Can. 199, par. 2.

22. *De Sponsal, et Matrim.,* II, page 236.

23. The jurisdiction of canon 1043 is according to the same author likewise vicarious.

24. Canons 197, par. 2, 199, par. 1.

25. *Ius Matrim.,* page 43.

26. Cf. Vlaming, *op. cit.* II, page 37; De Smet, *op. cit.* II, page 237.

27. De Smet, *op. cit.* II, page 236, footnote 1; Chelodi, *Ius Matrim.,* page 38; Vlaming, *op. cit.* II, pp. 76, sqq.

28. Cf. Vlaming, *op. cit., ibid.*

28a. *Op. cit.,* (3rd ed.), vol. II, p. 36.

29. *Op. cit.* II, page 218, footnote 2.

30. Blat, *op. cit.,* III, page 546, ed. 1920, Chelodi, *Ius Matrim.,* page 38.

31. The first argument De Smet, *op. cit.,* loc. cit., brings in support of his opinion is that the "impediment" of clandestinity is not excluded from the "*census impedimentorum,*" presumably in the Code. In reply to this it could be said, with equal weight, that form is not included, by the Code, among the diriment impediments, and, undoubtedly with more weight, that form is treated separately (canons 1094, sqq.) and expressly distinguished in canons 1043, 1139, 1137.—The second argument of De Smet is that the Index of the Code refers to canon 1094, on form, in its enumeration of the diriment impediments. In reply to that argument it is hardly necessary to state that the Index, though of high authority, is a private compilation, and hence cannot be considered an authentic interpretation of the Code. Aside from this, it is not a definite matter, and, after a consideration of the question of diriment impediments in the Index, it does not appear to be even a likely matter, that the compiler of the Index wanted to classify "clandestinity" among the diriment impediments. The Index refers the reader for information concerning the thir-

teen impediments, treated in canons 1067 to 1080, explicitly to the respective canons. For information concerning "clandestinity," the Index does not refer explicitly to any canon of the Code, nor does it refer even in a general way to the "*Impedimenta,*" but it only asks the reader to look up "*Matrimonium,*" where brief mention is made of the present juridical aspect of the former "clandestinity" in the references to the Code's legislation on form.

32. Canon 1045, par. 3.

33. Thus a reply of The Commission for the Authentic Interpretation of the Canons of the Code, *Acta Apost. Sedis,* vol. XIII, page 177.

34. Chelodi, *Ius Matrim.,* page 38.

35. Thus Blat, *op. cit.* III, page 546, ed. 1920.

36. Canons 1133, sqq.

37. A comparison of this paragraph and canon 1137 seems to disprove the opinion of De Smet, discussed above, that the impediments referred to in canon 1044 and canon 1045 include defect of form.

38. Cf. D'Annibale, *Summa Theol. Mor.* I, n. 242, footnote 49: *Occultum accipere debemus quod adeo pauci et prudentes sciunt, ut reputari possit quasi nemo sciret; et quia res facti est, in estimatione boni viri esse debet.* Petrovits, *The New Church Law On Matrimony,* page 97.

39. Canon 1046: *Parochus aut sacerdos de quo in can.* 1044, *de concessa dispensatione pro foro externo Ordinarium loci statim certiorem faciat; eaque adnotetur in libro matrimoniorum.*

40. Blat thinks that only those dispensations that are granted in virtue of canon 1044, that is, in danger of death, for the external forum, must be reported to the local Ordinary. *Op. cit.* III, page 547.

## XIV

## FACULTAS PRAEDICANDI VERBUM DEI

No one is allowed to exercise the ministry of preaching unless he has special permission from a competent Superior, or unless he has an office to which the law has attached the "*munus praedicandi.*"[1] The law requires now, as formerly, that the preacher receive the *missio*. The *missio* is given in the form of a "*facultas peculiariter data*" by the local Ordinary, or, as the case may be, by the religious Superior. The *missio* is, unless otherwise expressly stated, contained in the appointment to a position in the diocese to which the office of preaching is attached by the Code. Parish priests are not only permitted but obliged to preach on Sundays and feast days of obligation.[2] Assistant priests, likewise, have the right and obligation to preach "*nisi aliud expresse caveatur.*"[3] As far as pastors and assistants in their territory are concerned, the above stated faculty would not have to be placed in the document of diocesan faculties. But for other priests, who have no office in the diocese, and for parish priests and assistants outside their territory, the mention of the faculty of preaching is important, since the Code explicitly forbids preaching without a special faculty. This faculty includes the right to give catechetical instructions, unless the concession of the Ordinary expressly exempts this permission.

It is stated in canon 1337 and implied in 1341, par. 2, that the power to grant the faculty of preaching in the diocese belongs to the Ordinary. There seems to be no substantial objection to the view that the Ordinary may grant the "*facultas concionandi*" through the agency of the rural deans or other priests to those who would meet the constituted requirements.

Those who have the right to preach, *concionandi*, by reason of their office, or by delegation, such as parish priests and their assistants, respectively, are not allowed to delegate that right to others.[4]

Canon 1333 makes ample provision for the proper exercise of the right to catechize: Par. 1, *Parochus in religiosa puerorum institutione potest, imo, si legitime sit impeditus, debet operam adhibere clericorum, in paroeciae territorio degentium, aut etiam, si necesse sit, piorum laicorum, potissimum illorum qui in pium sodalitium doctrinae christianae aliudve simile in paroecia erectum adscripti sint.*

Par. 2. *Presbyteri aliique clerici, nullo legitimo impedimento detenti, proprio parocho in hoc sanctissimo opere adiutores sunto, etiam sub poenis ab Ordinario infligendis.*

## Notes

### XIV

1. Can. 1328: *Nemini ministerium praedicationis licet exercere, nisi a legitimo Superiore missionem receperit, facultate peculiariter data, vel officio collato, cui ex sacris canonibus praedicandi munus inhaereat.*
2. Can. 1344, par. 1.
3. Can. 476, par. 6.
4. Can. 1337; Cf. can. 1341, par. 2.

## XV

## FACULTAS BENEDICENDI SOLLEMNITER IMAGINES SACRAS PUBLICAE VENERATIONI EXPONDENDAS

The solemn blessing of a statute, or picture, or group that represents sacred persons, places, things or events, is reserved by common law to the Ordinary.[1] It is question here only of such sacred images that are to be placed or erected for public veneration. There is no legislation that prescribes a blessing, private or solemn, for sacred images. But it is the obvious desire of the Church that some blessing should be given. Solemn blessing is that which is given "*cum concursu populi, cum pluribus ministris.*"[2]

The *reservation* of the solemn blessing of sacred images seems based on a decree of the S. Cong. Rit.,[3] though there is nothing stated in the decree that bears on the *solemnity.* This qualification is presupposed in functions of a public nature at which the Ordinary officiates. The Rituale Romanum enumerates the blessing of sacred images among those reserved to the bishop, or to those who have the necessary faculty. From an application of the principle enunciated in canon 2 of the Code to the legislation of canon 1279, par. 4, we may deduce that the private blessing of sacred images is no longer reserved to the bishop.[4]

## Notes

### XV

1. Can. 1279, par. 4: *Si imagines, publicae venerationi expositae, sollemniter benedicantur, haec benedictio Ordinario reservatur, qui tamen potest eam cuilibet sacerdoti committere.*
2. Wapelhorst, *op. cit.*, p. 497.
3. *Calaguritana et Calceaten,* May 17, 1760, n. 2457.
4. Cf. Rit. Rom., Tit. VIII, c. 20, sqq. and c. 25.

In connection with the matter just treated, the following note concerning the *blessing of rosaries* may be added. In reply to the question: *An liceat Episcopis communicare presbyteris suae ditionis habitualiter potestatem benedicendi rosaria, etc., de qua in canone* 349, *par.* 1, *n.* 1, *cum applicatione indulgentiarum, observatis ritibus ab Ecclesia praescriptis* the S. Poentitentiaria gave a negative decision. . . . It would, no doubt, meet the desire of many a priest if the faculty of blessing rosaries and attaching indulgences to them were again obtained and inserted in the document of diocesan faculties.

## XVI

## FACULTAS DISPENSANDI ET COMMUTANDI, DUMMODO NE LAEDATUR IUS ALIIS QUAESITUM, OMNIA VOTA PRIVATA, EXCEPTIS VOTO PERFECTAE AC PERPETUAE CASTITATIS, ET VOTO INGREDIENDI IN RELIGIONEM VOTORUM SOLLEMNIUM, QUAE EMISSA FUERINT ABSOLUTE ET POST COMPLETUM DECIMUM OCTAVUM AETATIS ANNUM.

---

The Code defines a "public" vow as one that is accepted by a legitimate ecclesiastical Superior in the name of the Church. If a vow is not so accepted, it is a "private" vow.[1] This definition of the Code has settled definitely the uncertain distinction between public and private vows. The Code does not state that all public vows, whether solemn or simple (Can. 1308, par. 2), are reserved to the Holy See, but it does legislate that, of the private vows, only the two exceptions mentioned above in the diocesan faculty are reserved to the Holy See.

The dispensatory power of the Ordinary, which he could delegate to his priests in the diocesan faculty given above, is based on canon 1313, n. 1. The concession there mentioned reads as follows: *Vota non reservata possunt iusta de causa dispensare, dummodo dispensatio ne laedat ius aliis quaesitum*: 1.° *Loci Ordinarius quod attinet ad omnes suos subditos atque etiam peregrinos.*[2]

A dispensation from a vow means: *absoluta eius condonatio nomine Dei a legitimo Superiore facta.* A commutation of a vow is defined: *substitutio alicuius operis operi promisso.* He who has the power of dispensation from vows has also the power of commutation, but not *vice versa.*[3]

The dispensation or the commutation may not be granted if the rights of a third party are thereby violated. A decree of the Holy Office, Aug. 2, 1876,[4] explains this point clearly when it states that a bishop may dispense from certain vows *"dummodo ius ex contractu oneroso acquisitum tertii, ipso rationabiliter invito, non laedatur."*[5]

The first exception is the vow of perfect and perpetual chastity. Perfect chastity is that *"quae se continet ab omnibus delectationibus carnis etiam licitis in matrimonio."*[6] The second exception is the vow of entering a religious institute of solemn vows, namely an *"ordo"* or *"religio in qua vota sollemnia nuncupantur."*[7]

The reservation of these exceptions depends on two qualifications: 1) the vows must have been made without any conditions whatever; 2) the vows must have been made after the completion of the eighteenth year. Since a reservation is something *odiosum,* the two qualifications are to be interpreted strictly.

A sufficient cause must always be had before the dispensation or commutation can be granted. Serious difficulty in observing the obligations of the vow, grave anxiety or scrupulosity, well founded doubt about the binding force of the vow because of lack of deliberation or peace of mind at the time the vow was made, are considered adequate reasons.[8]

*Confessarii regulares* can dispense by reason of direct or communicated privileges from all non-reserved vows.[9]

## Notes

### XVI

1. Can. 1308, par. 1.

2. The expression "*vota non reservata*" suggests the question whether the simple vows of poverty and obedience in non-cloistered religious institutes, that have not as yet received the approval of the Holy See, are still "*vota non reservata.*" There seems to be no objection deducible from the Code against the view that these simple vows are still "*non reservata.*" To say the least, the bishop may, because of the "*dubium iuris,*" dispense from these vows, *ex potestate ordinaria.* Cf. Augustine, *op. cit.* VI, pp. 303, sqq.

3. *Regula Iuris,* 53 in 6to: *Cui licet quod est plus, licet utique quod est minus.*—Wernz, *op. cit.* III, 2, n. 584, sq.

4. *Collectanea* S. Cong. de Prop. Fide, n. 1461.

5. Cf. S. Alphonsus, *op. cit.* IV, n. 255.

6. Cf. Noldin, *De Sexto Praecepto,* nn. 1, sqq.

7. Can. 488, n. 2.

8. Cf. S. Alphonsus, *op. cit.* IV, nn. 250, sqq.

9. S. Alphonsus, *op. cit.* IV, n. 257; Augustine, *op. cit.* VI, pp. 306, sqq.; Sebastiani, *Summarium Theol. Mor.*, ed. 1919, n. 211.

## XVII

## DISPENSANDI AB IRREGULARITATIBUS OMNIBUS EX DELICTO OCCULTO PROVENIENTIBUS, EXCEPTIS ILLIS QUAE, ETSI PROPTER COOPERATIONEM TANTUM, EX HOMICIDIO VOLUNTARIO VEL EX ABORTU, EFFECTU SECUTO, ORIUNTUR, ET OMNIBUS AD FORUM IUDICIALE DEDUCTIS.

This faculty is based on canon 990, par. 1, which reads as follows: *Licet Ordinariis per se vel per alium suos subditos dispensare ab irregularitatibus omnibus ex delicto occulto provenientibus, ea excepta de qua in can.* 985, *n.* 4, *aliave deducta ad forum iudiciale.* The canon states expressly that the Ordinary may dispense from the irregularities mentioned therein through a delegated person, "*per alium.*" Hence, the Ordinary may place this delegated power among the concessions in the document of diocesan faculties.

The irregularities in question are only those that arise *ex delicto occulto,* and not those that arise *ex delicto publico* or *ex defectu.* Canon 985 enumerates the various classes of *delinquentes*: *Sunt irregulares ex delicto.* 1.° *Apostatae a fide, haeretici, schismatici;* 2.° *Qui, praeterquam in casu extremae necessitatis, baptismum ab acatholicis quovis modo sibi conferri siverunt;* 3.° *Qui matrimonium attentare aut civilem tantum actum ponere ausi sunt, vel ipsimet vinculo matrimoniali aut ordine sacro aut votis religiosis etiam simplicibus ac temporariis ligati, vel cum muliere iisdem votis adstricta aut matrimonio valido coniuncta;* 4.° *Qui voluntarium homicidium perpetrarunt aut fetus humani abortum procuraverunt, effectu secuto, omnesque cooperantes;* 5.° *Qui seipsos vel alios mutilaverunt vel sibi vitam adimere tentaverunt;* 6.° *Clerici medicam vel chirurgicam artem sibi vetitam exercentes, si exinde mors sequatur;* 7.° *Qui actum ordinis, clericis in ordine sacro constitutis reservatum, ponunt, vel eo ordine carentes, vel ab eius exercitio poena canonica sive personali, medicinali aut vindicativa, sive locali prohibiti.*

The meaning of the term *delictum occultum* in the question of irregularities may be gained from canon 2197, which defines *delictum occultum* as the opposite of *delictum publicum.* The latter is described in the following terms: *Delictum est publicum, si iam divulgatum est aut talibus contigit seu versatur in adiunctis ut prudenter iudicari possit et debeat facile divulgatum iri.* Since canon 990 does not distinguish between a crime that is materially occult and a crime that is formally occult, the concession granted by the canon would hold good even if the crime were only formally occult[1] as long as it were not brought before the *forum iudiciale.*

Voluntary homicide gives rise to an irregularity that is beyond the power of dispensation granted in canon 990. Casual or necessary homicide does not cause irregularity.[2] Hence, there is no irregularity arising from killing a person by accident (e. g. automobile accident, hunting, etc.) or in self-defense. The opinion seems tenable that culpable negligence resulting in homicide cannot be classified under the heading of voluntary homicide.[3] The Council of Trent,[4] in legislating on this matter uses "*voluntarium*" and "*ex proposito*" synonymously. . . Attempted suicide is not classified under voluntary homicide.[5]

The irregularity arising from abortion, likewise, is an exception referred to in canon 990, par. 1. Attempted or unsuccessful abortion is not a source of irregularity because of the requisite "*effectu secuto.*"[6]

Cooperation with either of the crimes here considered, homicide or abortion, makes the delinquent irregular. This irregularity is also beyond the grant of canon 990. Blat holds that the cooperation is to be judged from canon 2209 "*dummodo hi* (*scl. cooperantes*) *positivam dent operam delictum homicidii vel abortus principaliter patranti.*"[7] It matters not whether the positive help is contributed directly or indirectly to the principal agent.

The dispensatory power of canon 990, and of the faculty given above, does not cover irregularities arising from an occult crime that has been brought before the iudicial forum, civil or ecclesiastical.[8]

Common law grants to every confessor, even if he has not received the above faculty, the concession mentioned therein, but only for the more urgent occult cases in which the local Ordinary cannot be reached and in which, concurrently, there is imminent danger of "*grave damnum vel infamia.*" This concession is to be used by the confessor only for the purpose of dispensing those who are to exercise orders already received. The term "*confessarius*" and "*poenitens*" imply that the faculty is to be used in the internal sacramental forum only. Although the concession granted the Ordinary in canon 990, par. 1, refers to "*suos subditos,*" the concession granted the confessor in can. 990, par. 2, comprehends—*salvo meliori iudicio*—also "*extranei,*" because of the consideration that they become subjects of the Ordinary through the confessor.[9]

It is to be noted that the diocesan faculty may be used to dispense both *ordinati* and *ordinandi*, but that the faculty based on canon 990, par. 2, i. e. granted the confessor by common law, refers to the *ordinati* only.

For dispensations from irregularities not covered by the concessions of canon 990, recourse must be had, for the internal forum, sacramental and extra-sacramental, to the S. Penitentiary, for the external forum, to the Congregation on the discipline of the Sacraments, with the following exceptions: 1) to the Congregation for the Oriental Church for its subjects; 2) to the S. Congregation for the Propagation of the Faith for its subjects; 3) to the S. Congregation for Religious in cases of religious. . . In applying for dispensations the prescripts of canon 991 are to be observed: 1) *In precibus pro irregularitatum ac impedimentorum dispensatione, omnes irregularitates ac impedimenta indicanda sunt; secus dispensatio generalis valebit quidem etiam pro reticitis bona fide, iis exceptis quae in can.* 990, *par.* 1, *excipiuntur, non autem pro reticitis in mala fide.* 2) *Si agatur de irregularitate ex homicidio voluntario, etiam numerus delictorum exprimendus est sub poena nullitatis concedendae dispensationis.* 3) *Dispensatio generalis ad ordines valet pro ordinibus quoque maioribus; et dispensatus potest obtinere beneficia non consistorialia etiam curata, sed renuntiari nequit S. R. E. Cardinalis, Episcopus, Abbas vel Praelatus nullius, Superior maior in religione clericali exempta.* 4) *Dispensatio, in foro interno non sacramentali concessa, scripto consignetur; et de ea in secreto Curiae libro constare debet.*

It is of importance to remember that a dispensation, also when granted in virtue of the diocesan faculty, for the internal extra-sacramental forum, must be put down in writing and sent to the Curia, where it is to be kept in a secret book.

In granting a dispensation from an irregularity a formula may be used such as: *Ego te dispenso ab irregularitate (irregularitatibus) quam (quas) contraxisti ex* . . . . . . . . .[10]

## Notes

### XVII

1. Can. 2197, n. 4.
2. Blat, *Comment. Text. Iur. Can.*, III, p. 438.
3. Cf. Gasparri, *De Sacra Ordinatione*, n. 414.
4. *Sess.* XIV, *de ref.* c. 7.
5. Can. 985, n. 5.
6. Cf. Solc, *De Delictis et Poenis*, p. 316, sqq.
7. *Op. cit.* III, p. 439, ed. 1920.
8. Cf. Hickey, *Irregularities and Simple Impediments*, p. 87, sq.
9. The delegated power granted in the dioccsan faculty cannot be used, in the extra-sacramental forum, to dispense "*sacerdotes extranei*" from an irregularity.
10. Cf. Gasparri, *op. cit.*, n. 213.

## XVIII

## FACULTAS DISPENSANDI, IN CASIBUS SINGULARIBUS IUSTAQUE DE CAUSA, SINGULOS FIDELES SINGULASVE FAMILIAS A LEGE COMMUNI DE OBSERVANTIA FESTORUM ITEMQUE DE OBSERVANTIA ABSTINENTIAE ET IEIUNII VEL ETIAM UTRIUSQUE.

In virtue of canon 1245, par. 1, local Ordinaries and parish priests possess ordinary jurisdiction for dispensing their subjects, also outside their territory, and strangers, in their territory (i. e. of the Ordinaries and parishes, respectively), from the general law of feasts, fasts and abstinence. Although the parish priests have this power by common law and can delegate it to their assistants for their parishes, still it would be more convenient to have the concession embodied in the terms of a diocesan faculty. Then parish priests and assistants could use the concession in any parish of the diocese where their services might be required.

The faculty is applicable in individual cases only. Only individual persons or families may be dispensed in virtue thereof. Even the Ordinary himself could not grant a general dispensation from the observance of the feasts except according to the norm of canon 81. He could, however, grant a general dispensation from the law of fast or abstinence, or of both, "*ex causa peculiari magni populi concursus aut publicae valetudinis.*"[1] In view of the spirit of the law, indicated in canon 1252, par.

4, we do not think that the celebration of a patronal feast would constitute a *"causa peculiaris magni populi concursus."*

The powers that have been granted in the particular indults concerning the law of fast and abstinence have not been changed by the Code,[2] nor have they been revoked by the *Proxima sacra.*[3] The latter revoked only those indults that were contained *"vel in Brevi dicto* 25 *annorum, vel in formulis typis impressis ad decennium, ad quinquennium aut etiam triennium valituris."*

A just cause is required for granting the dispensations mentioned in the diocesan faculty. The cause is just when the degree of necessity for the exception to the law is equal to the degree of importance of the law's observance.[4] In doubt as to whether the cause is sufficiently proportionate to the importance of the law, the faculty may be used without any scruple.[5] The various causes for granting the dispensations under consideration need not be mentioned here since they are extensively treated in text-books of moral theology.

## Notes

### XVIII

1. Can. 1245, par. 2.
2. Can. 1253.
3. S. Cong. Consist., April 25, 1918.
4. Can. 84, par. 1.
5. Can. 84, par. 2.

# BIBLIOGRAPHY

## I

## SOURCES AND PERIODICALS

Acta Apostolicae Sedis.
Acta Sanctae Sedis.
American Ecclesiastical Review.
Analecta Ecclesiastica.
Archiv fuer katholisches Kirchenrecht. (A K R.)
Bullarium Romanum.
Canoniste Contemporain, Le.
Catholic Encyclopedia, The.
Codex Iuris Canonici.
Collectanea S. Congregationis de Prop. Fide.
Commentarium pro Religiosis (Rome).
Concilii Plenarii Baltimorensis III Acta et Decreta.
Concilii Tridentini Canones et Decreta.
Corpus Iuris Canonici (Richter-Friedberg, vol. I, 1879, vol. II, 1881, Leipsic).
Homiletic and Pastoral Reviews, The.
Irish Ecclesiastical Record, The.
Iuris Pontificii de Prop. Fide.
Kirchenlexikon (Herder).
Nouvelle Revue Théologique.
Theologisch-praktische Quartalschrift (Linz).
Zeitschrift fuer katholichse Theologie. (Z K T.)

## II.

### *Authors.*

Aguilar, *Institutiones Iuris Canonici* (*S. Dominici Calceat.*), 1904.

Alphonsus, S., *Theol. Mor.*, Ratisbonae, 1846.

D'Annibale, *Commentarium in Constit. Apost. Sedis*, Prati, 1894.

D'Annibale, *Summa Theol. Mor.*, 3 vols., Rome, 1891.

Arregui, *Summarium Theol. Mor.*, Oniae, 1919.

Augustine, *A Commentary on Canon Law,* St. Louis, 1918, sqq.

Baart, *The Roman Court,* 4th ed., New York, 1899.

Bachofen, *Compendium Iuris Regularium,* New York, 1903.

Bargilliat, *Droits et Devoirs des Curés et des Vicaires paroissiaux,* Paris, 1919.

Bargilliat, *Praelectiones Iuris Canonici,* vol. I, Paris, 1921.

Blat, *Comment. Textus Iuris Canonici,* vols. I, II, III, Rome, 1920, 1921.

Bouix, *De Iure Regularium,* 2 vols., Paris, 1882.

Cappello, *De Censuris,* Turin, 1919.

Cappello, *De Sacramentis,* vol. I, Turin, 1921.

Cerato, *Matrimonium,* Patavii, 1918.

Chelodi, *Ius Matrimoniale,* Tridenti, 1921.

Chelodi, *Ius Poenale,* Tridenti, 1920.

Cocchi, *Comment. in Codicem Iuris Canonici,* vol. I, Turin, 1920.

De Smet, *De Sponsalibus et Matrimonio,* 2 vols., Bruges, 1920.

De Smet, *Praxis Matrimonialis,* Bruges, 1920.

Fanfani, *De Iure Religiosorum,* Turin, 1920.

Frericks, *Religious Congregations in Their External Relations,* Washington, 1916.

Gasparri, *De Eucharistia,* 2 vols., Paris, 1897.

Gasparri, *De Matrimonio,* 2 vols., Paris, 1904.

Gasparri, *De Sacra Ordinatione,* 2 vols., Paris, 1893.

Goeller, *Die paepstliche Poenitentiarie,* Rome, 1907.
Hickey, *Irregularities and Simple Impediments,* Washington, 1920.
Hollweck, *Kirchliche Strafgesetze,* Mainz, 1899.
Klekotka, *Diocesan Consultors,* Washington, 1920.
Konings, *Comment. in Facultates Apostolicas,* New York, 1884.
Konings-Putzer, *Commentarium in Facultates Apost.,* 4th ed., New York, 1897.
Kubelbeck, *The Sacred Penitentiaria and its Relations to Faculties of Ordinaries and Priests,* Washington, 1918.
Leitner, *Handbuch des kath. Kirchenrechts,* Regensburg, 1918.
Mergentheim, *Die Quinquennalfakultaeten pro foro externo,* vol. II, Stuttgart, 1908.
Morino, *Theologia Moralis,* 2 vols., Naples, 1910.
Munerati, *Iuris Eccl. Publici et Privati Elementa,* Rome, 1920.
Noldin, *Summa Theol. Moralis,* 3 vols., Innsbruck, 1914.
Noval, *De Processibus,* Rome, 1920.
Ojetti, *De Romana Curia,* Rome, 1910.
Ojetti, *Synopsis Rerum Mor. et Iuris Pontificii,* Rome, 1912.
Papi, *The Government of Religious Communities,* New York, 1919.
Papi, *Religious Profession,* New York, 1918.
Petrovits, *The New Church Law on Matrimony,* Philadelphia, 1919.
Pirhing, *Ius Canonicum,* Dilingen, 1772.
Putzer (cf. supra Konings-Putzer).
Reiffenstuel, *Ius Canonicum,* Venice, 1775.
Rodericus, *Resolutiones Questionum Regularium,* Lugdini, 1634.

Sabetti-Barret, *Theol. Moralis,* 1902, 1919, New York.

Schaaf, *The Cloister,* Washington, 1921.

Schmalzgrueber, *Ius Eccl.,* Rome, 1845.

Schulte, *Geschichte der Quellen u. Litteratur d. Can. Rechts,* 3 vols., Stuttgart, 1875.

Sebastianelli, *De Personis,* Rome, 1905.

Sebastiani, *Summarium Theol. Moralis,* Turin, 1919.

Sole, *De Delictis et Poenis,* Rome, 1920.

Suarez, *Opera Omnia,* Paris, 1856.

Tanquerey, *Synopsis Theol. Mor. et Pastor.,* Rome, 1920.

Vermeersch, *De Religiosis,* Bruges, 1911, sqq.

Vlaming, *Praelectiones Iuris Matrimonii,* 2 vols., Bussum, 1919.

Wernz, *Ius Decretalium,* 6 vols., Prati, 1913.

Zitelli, *Apparatus Iuris Canonici,* Rome, 1888.

UNIVERSITAS CATHOLICA AMERICAE

WASHINGTONII, D. C.

SACRA FACULTAS THEOLOGICA

1921-1922

No. 16

# CANONES

DEUS LUX MEA

---

# CANONES

QUOS

AD DOCTORATUS GRADUM

IN

# IURE CANONICO

Apud Universitatem Catholicam Americae

CONSEQUENDUM

PUBLICE PROPUGNABIT

HUBERTUS LUDOVICUS MOTRY

Sacerdos Dioecesis Albanensis

SACRAE THEOLOGIAE DOCTOR

ET

IURIS CANONICI LICENTIATUS

HORA XI A. M., DIE XXIX MAII, A. D. MCMXXII

## LIB. I.

Canones.

I. 1-7 Praeliminaria.
II. 8-9 De promulgatione legum ecclesiasticarum.
III. 17-19 De interpretatione legum ecclesiasticarum.
IV. 25-30 De consuetudine.
V. 31-35 De supputatione temporis.
VI. 49-50 De intepretatione rescriptorum.
VII. 66 De facultatibus habitualibus.
VIII. 63-65 De acquisitione privilegiorum.
IX. 71-78 De extinctione privilegiorum.
X. 80-86 De dispensationibus.

## LIB. II.

XI. 111-117 De clericorum adscriptione alicui dioecesi.
XII. 118-123 De iuribus et privilegiis clericorum.
XIII. 142 De negotiatione clericis prohibita.
XIV. 196-210 De potestate ordinaria et delegata.
XV. 271-280 De Patriarchis, Primatibus, Metropolitis.
XVI. 366-371 De vicario Generali.
XVII. 471-478 De vicariis paroecialibus.
XVIII. 423-428 De consultoribus dioecesanis.
XIX. 522, 523 De quibusdam confessariis religiosarum.
XX. 673-681 De societatibus sive virorum sive mulierum in communi viventium sine votis.

## LIB. III.

XXI. 755-761 De ritibus et caeremoniis baptismi.
XXII. 804 De admittendo sacerdote extraneo ad missae celegrationem.
XXIII. 806 De binatione.

XXIV. 820-823 De tempore et loco Missae celebrandae.
XXV. 882 De absolutione in periculo mortis.
XXVI. 884 De absolutione complicis.
XXVII. 894, 904 De sollicitatione.
XXVIII. 908-910 De loco ad confessiones excipiendas.
XXIX. 938, 939 De ministro extremae unctionis.
XXX. 990, 991 De dispensatione ab irregularitatibus.
XXXI. 1043-1046 De quibusdam dispensationibus matrimonialibus.
XXXII. 1133-1137 Deconvalidatione simplici.
XXXIII. 1138-1141 De sanatione in radice.
XXXIV. 1171-1175 De violatione ecclesiae.
XXXV. 1250-1254 De abstinentia et ieiunio.
XXXVI. 1274, 1275 De cultu SS. Eucharistiae.
XXXVII. 1279-1281 De cultu S. Imaginum.
XXXVIII. 1307-1315 De voto.
XXXIX. 1364-1366 De ratione studiorum in Seminariis.
XL. 1385-1394 De praevia censura librorum.

LIB. IV.

XLI. 1572-1579 De Iudice.
XLII. 1585-1590 De Notario, Promotore iustitiae, vinculi Defensore.
XLIII. 1594-1596 De tribunali ordinario secundae instantiae.
XLIV. 1667-1671 De actionibus et exceptionibus.
XLV. 1701-1705 De extinctione actionum.
XLVI. 1750-1753 De confessione partium.
XLVII. 1825-1828 De praesumptionibus.
XLVIII. 1892-1897 De querela nullitatis contra sententiam iudicialem.
XLIX. 1960-1992 De causis matrimonialibus.
L. 2162-2167 De modo procedendi in translatione parochorum.

LIB. V.

LI. 2195-2198 De natura delicti eiusque divisione.
LII. 2215-2219 De poenarum notione, speciebus, interpretatione atque applicatione.
LIII. 2253, 2254 De absolutione a censura extra periculum mortis.
LIV. 2303-2305 De depositione, privatione habitus, degradatione.
LV. 2320-2329 De delictis contra religionem.
LVI. 2350, 2351 De delictis contra vitam.
LVII. 2360-2363 De crimine falsi.
LVIII. 2364-2375 De delictis in administratione vel susceptione Sacramentorum.
LIX. 2376-2389 De delicitis contra obligationes proprias status clericalis vel religiosi.
LX. 2404-2414 De abusu potestatis vel officii eccelestiastici.

Vidit Sacra Facultas:
CAROLUS F. AIKEN, S. T. D., p. t. Decanus,
HENRICUS SCHUMACHER, S. T. D., p. t. a Secretis.

Vidit Rector Universitatis:
†THOMAS J. SHAHAN, S. T. D., J. U. L.

# BIOGRAPHY

Hubert Louis Motry was born August 28, 1884, in Tiffin, Ohio. He received his elementary education at St. Joseph's Parochial School of the same city, his college and seminary course at the Pontificial College Josephinum, Columbus, Ohio, where he was ordained priest by the Rt. Rev. James J. Hartley, 1909. For eight years he was a member of the teaching faculty of the Josephinum. In 1917 he entered The Catholic University of America, Washington, D. C., and pursued theological studies under the direction of Dr. John A. Ryan, Dr. Edmund T. Shanahan and Monsignor Dr. Phillipp Bernardini, to all of whom he hereby expresses his sincere thanks.

www.ingramcontent.com/pod-product-compliance
Lightning Source LLC
LaVergne TN
LVHW050228080826
844660LV00012B/494
*9780813222073*